English Without Mistakes

عربى

Shawki Saadel Din Mohammed

اسـم الكتـاب :Shawki Saad Eldin Mohamed/ إنجليزيه بدون أخطاء =

English without mistakes

اسـم المؤلـف : Shawki Saad Eldin ،Mohamed

رقـم الإيـداع : 2011/5117

الترقيم الدولى : 5 644 277 977 978

للنشر والتوزيع والتصدير

42 شارع علي أمين امتداد مصطفى النحاس ـ
مدينة نصر ـ القاهرة
تليفون: 24015278 - 24015279 (202)
فاكس: 24043803 (202)
E-mail : info@altalae.com
Web site: www.altalae.com

تصميم الغلاف الفنان: إبراهيم محمد

تطلب جميع مطبوعاتنا من وكيلنا الوحيد بالمملكة العربية السعودية

مكتبة الساعي للنشر والتوزيع

ص.ب 50649 الرياض 11533 ـ هاتف: 4353768 ـ 4351966 ـ 4359066
فاكس: 4355945   جوال: 0550671967
جدة: هاتف/ فاكس: 6294367   جوال: 0550671976
E-mail: alsaay99@hotmail.com

مطابع العبور الحديثة - القاهرة
تليفون: 46651013 فاكس: 46651599

إعادة طبع Reprint
2011

مقدمة

يواجه الدارس للغة الإنجليزية فى العالم العربى، الكثير من الصعوبات فى طريق إجادته لها. ومن هذا المنطلق كان من الضرورى البحث والتدقيق من خلال الممارسة العملية للغة بكافة أشكال استخداماتها إلى جانب القراءات العديدة حول الأخطاء الشائعة بين الدارسين للغة، لكى أخرج بهذا الكتاب والذى استطعت من خلاله أن أعرض خلاصة التجربة فى اللغة الإنجليزية من خلال أسلوب يسهل على أى دارس - سواء أكان طالبا أو دارسا للغة بوجه عام - معرفة الأخطاء التى يقع فيها معظم دارسي اللغة لكى يصححها، أو يتجنبها عند استخدامه للغة، سواء أكان ذلك فى النطق أو التركيب اللغوى أو الكتابة بمعناها ومبناها الواسعين.

وكم يراودنى الأمل أن يكون هذا الجهد المتواضع شعلة فى طريق النجاح لأى دارس يريد أن يعرف أسرار اللغة، ويغوص فى أعماق البناء اللغوى بدءًا من الكلمة إلى الجملة بكافة أشكالها.

المؤلف

Spelling
الهجاء

نظرًا لصعوبة الهجاء في اللغة الإنجليزية خاصة بالنسبة للدارس المبتدئ وجدنا أنه من الضروري إعداد هذا الفصل من كتابنا. وسوف يجد الدارس أننا قد أعددناه بصورة قواعد للهجاء في اللغة الإنجليزية تصل إلى حوالي 36 قاعدة.

وننهي هذا الفصل بفرع ثان بملاحظات عامة في الهجاء ربما لا تخضع لقاعدة معينة.

ثم لاحظنا أيضًا وجود صعوبة في التمييز بين الكلمات التي تقترب في النطق والهجاء وتختلف في المعنى، لذلك كان من الضروري عند الحديث عن الهجاء أن نبين ذلك في فرع آخر من هذا الفصل في صورة جدول يبين بعض الكلمات الشائعة في هذا الخصوص.

وسوف يجد الدارس أن هناك إمكانية لوضع قواعد للهجاء في اللغة الإنجليزية على غير الشائع، إلا أنه من الجدير بالذكر أن هذه القواعد مجرد شعلة تنير لك في بداية السير في دروب اللغة التي سوف تكتسبها أكثر فأكثر مع كثرة المطالعة والتعامل. متمنين لك بعد دراسة هذه القواعد أن تكسبك Sense (الإحساس) بهجاء الكلمات الإنجليزية.

ENGLISH
WITHOUT
MISTAKES

متفرقات:

بالنسبة لكلمات التى تحتوى على (i) و (e) فإنه :

- تأتى i قبل e فى أغلب الأحوال مثل :

believe يعتقد و grief حزن

- تأتى i بعد e فى الحالات الآتية :

(1) إذا جاء الحرفان i,e بعد c مثل

Receive يتسلم و Ceiling سقف

(2) عندما تنطق e على أنها (a) مثل

Neighbor جار وكلمة ، Weight وزن

ولكن توجد بعض الاستثناءات مثل :

foreign أجنبي - height ارتفاع - neither ولا أحد - leisure راحة

عند الإشارة إلى ضمير الغائب للأفعال التى تنتهى بـ

ch - sh - s - ss - x أضف es بدلاً من s :

he watches - يشاهد watch

she washes - يغسل wash

she mixes - يخلط mix

he passes - يمر pass

it matches - يلائم match

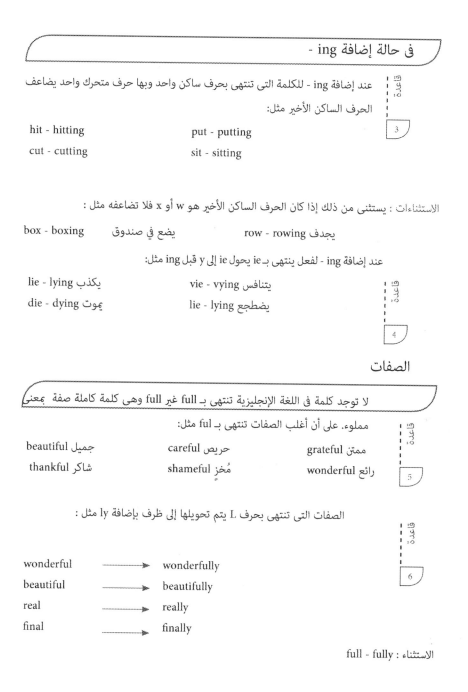

- في حالة إضافة ing

عند إضافة ing - للكلمة التي تنتهي بحرف ساكن واحد وبها حرف متحرك واحد يضاعف الحرف الساكن الأخير مثل:

hit - hitting	put - putting
cut - cutting	sit - sitting

قاعدة 3

الاستثناءات : يستثنى من ذلك إذا كان الحرف الساكن الأخير هو w أو x فلا تضاعفه مثل :

box - boxing يضع في صندوق	row - rowing يجدف

عند إضافة ing - لفعل ينتهي بـ ie يحول إلى y قبل ing مثل:

lie - lying يكذب	vie - vying يتنافس
die - dying يموت	lie - lying يضطجع

قاعدة 4

الصفات

لا توجد كلمة في اللغة الإنجليزية تنتهى بـ full غير full وهى كلمة كاملة صفة بمعنى

مملوء. على أن أغلب الصفات تنتهى بـ ful مثل:

beautiful جميل	careful حريص	grateful ممتن
thankful شاكر	shameful مُخزٍ	wonderful رائع

قاعدة 5

الصفات التى تنتهى بحرف L يتم تحويلها إلى ظرف بإضافة ly مثل :

قاعدة 6

wonderful	⟶	wonderfully
beautiful	⟶	beautifully
real	⟶	really
final	⟶	finally

الاستثناء : full - fully

قاعدة ٧: عند إضافة مقطع أخير للصفات التى تنتهى بـ y تبقى y كما هى مثل :

dry جاف - dryly

sly خبيث-ماكر - slyly

shy خجول - shyly

قاعدة ٨: عند إضافة ous لكلمات تنتهى بـ ce تتحول e إلى i قبل ous مثل:

grace رحمة - gracious رحيم

space سعة - spacious واسع

malice حقد - malicious حقود

vice رذيلة - vicious رذيل

قاعدة ٩: غالباً عندما تنتهى الصفة ذات المقطع الواحد بحرف ساكن يسبقه حرف متحرك ، فإن إضافة مقطع جديد يضاعف الحرف الساكن الأخير . مثل :

big كبير - bigger

hot ساخن - hotter

fit لائق - fitter

استثناءات مثل : low - lower

قاعدة ١٠: فى الصفات التى تنتهى بـ er أو ow ولا يستخدم معها more أو most يضاف إليها er أو est عند تحويلها إلى حالتي المقارنة مثل :

clever ماهر - cleverer - cleverest

narrow ضيق - narrower - narrowest

قاعدة ١١: إذا انتهت الصفة بـ le نضيف إلى نهايتها r - أو st عند تحويلها إلى حالتي المقارنة مثل:

gentle لطيف - gentler - gentlest

noble نبيل/ شهم - nobler - noblest

عند تحويل الصفة ذات المقطع الواحد - التى تنتهى بـ y يسبقه حرف متحرك - إلى ظرف ،
تحذف الـ y ونضع ily مثل :

gay مرح- gaily

day يوم - daily

التحويل للفعل الماضى بإضافة ed

عند تحويل الفعل (المصدر) إلى الزمن الماضى وينتهى بـ e - نضيف فقط حرف d إلى نهاية
الفعل مثل :

live يعيش- lived   hope يأمل - hoped

عند تحويل الفعل المصدر إلى الزمن الماضى بإضافة ed إليه - وهذا الفعل ذو مقطعين والمقطع
الثانى مُشدد، وينتهى بحرف ساكن مسبوق بحرف متحرك - يضاعف الحرف الساكن الأخير عند
التحويل مثل :

regret يندم ⟶ regretted   prefer يفضل ⟶ preferred

fulfil ينجز ⟶ fulfilled

عند تحويل الفعل المصدر إلى الزمن الماضى بإضافة ed إليه - وينتهى بحرف ساكن مسبوق بحرف
متحرك - يضاعف الحرف الساكن، وذلك باستثناء الأفعال التى تنتهى بـ v-w-x-y-z : أمثلة :

stop ⟶ stopped   rub ⟶ rubbed

fit ⟶ fitted

الاستثناءات هى :

fix يثبت ⟶ fixed   play يلعب ⟶ played

mix يخلط ⟶ mixed

عند تحويل الفعل المصدر إلى الزمن الماضى بإضافة ed إليه ، وينتهى الفعل المصدر بـ y ، فإذا
كانت y مسبوقة بحرف متحرك تبقى كما هى عند التحويل مثل:

play يلعب ⟶ played   stay يبقى ⟶ stayed

sway يتمايل ⟶ swayed

أما إذا كانت y مسبوقة بحرف ساكن ، تحول y إلى i مثل :

study   ⟶   studied   fry   ⟶   fried

try   ⟶   tried

ملاحظة : تطبق نفس القاعدة على صيغة هذه الأفعال فى زمن المضارع ، مع ضمير الغائب

مثل :

play   ⟶   he plays   sway   ⟶   she sways

fry   ⟶   she fries   try   ⟶   he tries

(قواعد متفرقة)

قاعدة 17

يوجد فقط ثلاثة أفعال فى اللغة الإنجليزية تنتهى بـ eed وهى :

exceed - proceed - succeed

أما الأفعال الأخرى المشابهة تنطق بنفس الطريقة لكنها تنتهى بـ ede مثل :

precede - recede - concede - supersede

تضاعف الحرف عند التحويل من ... إلى...

قاعدة 18

الكلمات التى تنتهى بحرف n يتضاعف هذا الحرف عند إضافة ess كما هو مثل :

barren قاحل   barrenness

mean خسيس   meanness

keen فطن   keenness

plain واضح   plainness

قاعدة 19

فى أغلب الحالات عند إضافة مقطع أخير لكلمة تنتهى بحرف L مسبوق بحرف أو حرفين متحركين أو

منفصلين فى النطق يتضاعف حرف L مثل:

quarrel شجار	quarrelling
cruel قاس	cruelly
dial أدار القرص	dialling
model نموذج	modelling

* استثناء : هذا التغيير لا يحدث فى الإنجليزية الأمريكية:

quarrel	quarreling
dial	dialing
model	modeling

قاعدة 20

عند إضافة مقطع أخير لكلمة تنتهى بحرف ساكن يسبقه حرفان متحركان لا يتضاعف الحرف الأخير . مثل :

beat يهزم - beaten

greet يحيى - greeted

قاعدة 21

عند تحويل كلمة تنتهى بأكثر من حرف ساكن لا يتضاعف الحرف الأخير منها مثل:

help يساعد	helped
return يعود	returned
earn يكسب	earned

قاعدة 22

فى أغلب الحالات عند إضافة مقطع أخير يبدأ بحرف ساكن لفعل ينتهى بحرف e غير منطوقة تظل e كما هى بغير حذف مثل:

use يستخدم	useful
extreme يبالغ	extremely
love يحب	lovely
move يتحرك	movement
nine	ninety

هناك استثناءات لذلك مثل :

argue - argument

itemize - itemization

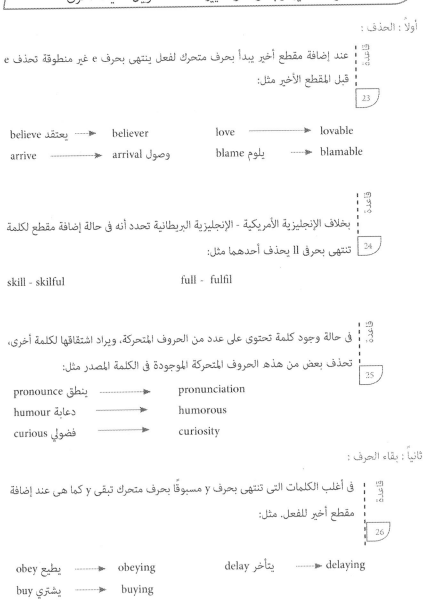

حذف الحرف الأخير أو بقاؤه أو تغييره عند التحويل لصيغة أخرى

أولاً: الحذف:

قاعدة 23

عند إضافة مقطع أخير يبدأ بحرف متحرك لفعل ينتهى بحرف e غير منطوقة تحذف e قبل المقطع الأخير مثل:

believe يعتقد ⟶ believer   love ⟶ lovable

arrive ⟶ arrival وصول   blame يلوم ⟶ blamable

قاعدة 24

بخلاف الإنجليزية الأمريكية - الإنجليزية البريطانية تحدد أنه فى حالة إضافة مقطع لكلمة تنتهى بحرف ll يحذف أحدهما مثل:

skill - skilful   full - fulfil

قاعدة 25

فى حالة وجود كلمة تحتوى على عدد من الحروف المتحركة، ويراد اشتقاقها لكلمة أخرى، تحذف بعض من هذه الحروف المتحركة الموجودة فى الكلمة المصدر مثل:

pronounce ينطق ⟶ pronunciation

humour دعابة ⟶ humorous

curious فضولى ⟶ curiosity

ثانياً: بقاء الحرف:

قاعدة 26

فى أغلب الكلمات التى تنتهى بحرف y مسبوقاً بحرف متحرك تبقى y كما هى عند إضافة مقطع أخير للفعل. مثل:

obey يطيع ⟶ obeying   delay يتأخر ⟶ delaying

buy يشترى ⟶ buying

هناك بعض الاستثناءات مثل :

pay ....⟶ paid   say ....⟶ said

lay ⟶ laid

قاعدة **27** عند إضافة مقطع أخير لكلمة تنتهى بحرفين ساكنين يظل الحرفان الساكنان كما هما بدون تغيير مثل :

embarrass يحرج ....⟶ embarrassment

success نجاح ....⟶ successful

assess يقيم ....⟶ assessment

قاعدة **28** عند إضافة مقطع أخير يبدأ بـ a أو o لكلمة تنتهى بـ ce أو ge تبقى e كما هى بدون حذف مثل :

peace ⟶ peaceably   courage ⟶ courageous

trace ⟶ traceable   replace ....⟶ replaceable

قاعدة **29** عند إضافة مقطع أخير لكلمات تنتهى بـ ee تبقى كما هى مثل :

agree ....⟶ agreement

foresee ⟶ foreseeable/ foreseeing

ثالثاً : تغيير الحرف الأخير :

قاعدة **30** عند إضافة أى مقطع ما عدا ing إلى كلمة تنتهى بـ y مسبوق بحرف ساكن يتحول الـ y إلى i مثل :

carry ....⟶ carried   happy ⟶ happiness

sunny ⟶ sunnier

أما فى حالة إضافة ing فتبقى y كما هى مثل:

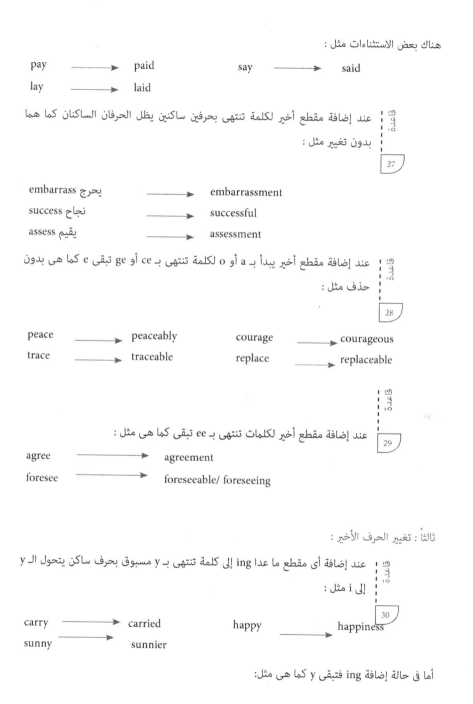

13   English without

| carry | -------------------------> | carrying |
| hurry | -------------------------> | hurrying |

(متفرقات)

يتبع حرف q الحرف المتحرك u فى أغلب الكلمات مثل:

quiet - unique - quake - quit - quote - quantity - quarry - quadratic - quench - quell

31

والاستثناءات غالباً لأسماء غير إنجليزية :

qiama - qibla - qintar

الإنجليزية البريطانية والإنجليزية الأمريكية

الأفعال التى تنتهى بـ ise فى الإنجليزية البريطانية ، يتم هجاؤها ize فى الإنجليزية الأمريكية مثل :

32

| organise | civilize | economise |
| organize | civilse | economize |

العديد من الكلمات التى تشتمل على (our) فى الإنجليزية البريطانية تكتب بدون حرف u فى الإنجليزية الأمريكية .

33

colour - color

flavour - flavor

العديد من الكلمات التى تنتهى بـ re فى الإنجليزية البريطانية يتم هجاؤها بـ er فى الإنجليزية الأمريكية.

34

إنجليزية بريطانية	إنجليزية أمريكية
centre	center
theatre	theater
litre	liter

العديد من الكلمات التى تنتهى بـ ce فى الإنجليزية البريطانية، يتم هجاؤها se فى الأمريكية:

إنجليزية بريطانية	إنجليزية أمريكية
defence دفاع	defense
offence إهانة	offense
pretence تظاهر	pretense

العديد من الكلمات التى تحتوى على ae و oe فى الإنجليزية البريطانية، يتم هجاؤها بدون a ، o فى الإنجليزية الأمريكية:

manoeuvre مناورة - maneuver

mediaeval من القرون الوسطى -medieval

التمييز بين بعض الكلمات فى الهجاء

الكلمة	المعنى
altar	مذبح للقرابين
alter	يبدل
adapt	يتكيف
adopt	يتبنى
allusion	تلميح
illusion	خداع
bread	خبز
bred	يربى ، يتوالد
bough	غصن كبير
bow	ينحنى
cell	خلية
sell	يبيع
contagious	مُعْدٍ
contiguous	مجاوِر

الكلمة	المعنى
ant	نملة
aunt	عمة
advise	ينصح
advice	نصيحة
analyse	يحلل
analysis	تحليل
breath	نفس
breathe	يتنفس
break	يكسر
brake	(فرامل)
complement	تكملة
compliment	مجاملة
cord	خيط غليظ
chord	وتر موسيقى

الكلمة	المعنى
councilor	عضو مجلس تشريعي
counselor	مستشار
casual	عرضي
causal	سببي
cannon	مدفع
canon	دستور
confident	واثق
confidential	سري
corps	فيلق
corpse	جثة الإنسان
command	يأمر
commend	يزكي
concur	يطابق
conquer	يغلب
disease	مرض
decease	موت
die	يموت
dye	صبغة
eligible	مؤهل
illegible	غير مقروء
except	فيما عدا
accept	يقبل

الكلمة	المعنى
credible	ممكن تصديقه
credulous	سريع التصديق ، ساذج
christen	يعمّد
christian	مسيحي
childish	غبي
childlike	بريء
continual	متكرر
continuous	مستمر
course	مسار
coarse	خشن - فظ
conscious	مدرك
conscience	الضمير
dairy	مصنع منتجات الألبان
diary	مفكرة
desert	صحراء
dessert	حلوى
effect	أثر
affect	يؤثر على
emigrate	يهاجر من بلده
immigrate	يهاجر إلى بلد آخر
expedite	يعجل
expedient	مناسب ، وسيلة

الكلمة	المعنى		الكلمة	المعنى
elicit	استخراج		elusive	صعب الإدراك
illicit	محرم		illusive	خادع
epigram	قول مأثور		exercise	يتمرن
epithet	صفة		exorcise	يطردالروح الشريرة
epitaph	قطعة تأبينية			
flower	زهرة		fowl	طائر
flour	دقيق		foul	قذر ، يلوث ، يفسد
facility	تسهيل ، سهولة		fare	أجرة سيارة
felicity	سعادة		fair	جميل
forth	الرابع		find	يجد
fourth	فصاعداً		fined	عاقب بغرامة
heal	يشفي		hear	يسمع
heel	كعب		hare	أرنب بري
hair	شعر		human	بشرى
here	هنا		humane	عطوف
heir	وريث - ولي العهد			
hole	فتحة			
hall	صالة			
whole	كل			
imminent	على وشك الحدوث		lesson	درس
eminent	رفيع المقام		lessen	يخفف
lead	يقود		lose	يفقد
lead	الرصاص		loose	مفكوك

الكلمة	المعنى	الكلمة	المعنى
lid	غطاء		
leak	يتسرب	lain	موضوع مطروح
leek	كلام قاس	laid	مستلق
lightning	برق	morning	صباح
lightening	تخفيف	mourning	حداد
pair	زوج	peace	السلام
pear	كمثرى	piece	جزء
pour	يصب	principal	أساسي
pore	ثقب	principle	قاعدة، مبدأ
profit	ربح	proposition	اقتراح
prophet	رسول	preposition	حرف جر
precis	خلاصة، تلخيص	penalty	عقوبة
precise	دقيق	penalise	يعاقب
pane	لوح الزجاج	peal	قصف الرعد
pain	ألم	peel	يقشر
pan	مقلاة		
pray	يصلى	proceed	يباشر، يواصل
prey	ضحية	precede	يتقدم، يسبق
prophesy	يتكهن	prospective	محتمل
prophecy	تنبأ	perspective	الشكل المنظورى
practise	يتمرن	quiet	هادىء
practice	تمرين	quite	تماماً
receipt	إيصال	rout	يهزم
recipe	وصفة طبية	route	طريق
raise	ينشئ	reign	تولى الملك

الكلمة	المعنى
rain	تمطر
rein	العنان ، اللجام
social	اجتماعي
sociale	أليف
scene	منظر، مشهد
seen	التصريف الثالث
sensible	عقلاني
sensitive	مرهف الإحساس
seize	يتولى
cease	يتوقف
sealing	إحكام السد
ceiling	سقف
throne	عرش
thrown	تصريف throw
their	ضمير الملكية
there	هناك
vain	متكبر
vane	دوارة الريح
vein	عرْق

الكلمة	المعنى
raze	يهدم -يدمر
write	يكتب
right	يمين
ritte	منسك
sea	بحر
see	يرى
sale	بيع
sail	يبحر
stationary	مستقر
stationery	قرطاسية
so	لأجل ، لذلك
sow	يزرع
temporal	علماني
temporary	مؤقت
to	حرف جر
too	أيضاً
two	رقم 2
thorough	متقن
through	عبر - من خلال
weather	مناخ
whether	إذا

Correct
pronunciation
النطق الصحيح

إننا حقا نعيش فى عصر المعلومات، سواء على المستوى الفردى، أو على مستوى المجتمعات وأصبحت اللغة الإنجليزية هى حجر الأساس فى نقل هذه المعلومات ، ولكى يتم تبادل المعلومات بصورة صحيحة ودقيقة فلابد أن يتم ذلك بنطق صحيح ، ومن هذا المنطلق جاء هذا الفصل ليعد مرجعاً للدارسين فى هذا المجال ، حيث تمت صياغته بأسلوب تعليمى منظم آخذين فى الاعتبار أن النطق الصحيح يعتمد فى الأساس على المخارج الصحيحة لحروف الكلمة، لذا اجتهدنا فى عرض بعض القواعد كمحاولة لمساعدة الدارسين على تلافى الأخطاء عند نطق الكلمات التى تتباين فى لفظها ، إلا أن ذلك لا يغنى عن سماع اللغة حيث أن علم اللغة هو علم صوتى ، علماً بأن مخارج الهجاء الصوتى لأحرف اللغة تختلف من لغة إلى أخرى، نظراً لاختلاف البيئة الثقافية ، فمخارج الألفاظ فى اللغة العربية تختلف عن مثيلاتها فى الإنجليزية ومن ثم نحذر من الهجاء الصوتى لأحرف اللغة الإنجليزية بنفس طريقة الصوت لأحرف اللغة العربية .

ENGLISH
WITHOUT
MISTAKES

(1) لا تنطق حرف k فى بداية الكلمات إذا تلاه حرف n مثل :

knowledge معرفة   عقدة/رباط knot

knee ركبة   سكين knife

knock يقرع

(2) لا تنطق حرف h إذا بدأت الكلمات بـ rh مثل :

rhythm إيقاع   rhyme كافية

rhomb معين هندسي   rhinoceros وحيد القرن

rhetorical بلاغي   rheumatism روماتيزم

(3) لا تنطق حرف h إذا كانت الكلمة تبدأ بـ gh مثل :

ghastly مروع   ghost شبح

gherkin خيار صغير   غول ghoul

ghetto الغيت

(4) فى معظم الكلمات التى تبدأ بحرف wh لا تنطق حرف h مثل :

where   سوط-كرباج whip

wheat قمح   when

الاستثناءات :

whole   whom   who

بينما الأمريكان ينطقون wh على أنه hw مثل :

when

(1) لا تنطق حرف g إذا تلاه حرف n فى بداية الكلمات :

gnat ناموس   صرير الأسنان gnash

gnaw نخر   المعرفة الصوفية gnosis

(5) لا تنطق حرف w عندما يأتي بعده حرف r في بعض الكلمات مثل :

انتزع wrest	تصارع wrestle
صعلوك wretch	معصم wrist
مصارعة wrestling	مشاحنة wrangle
	إكليل wreath

(6) لا تنطق حرف b في الكلمات التي تنتهي بـ mb مثل :

قبر tomb	قذيفة bomb
خروف lamb	مشط comb
	يتسلق climb

(7) أما في الكلمات التي تنتهي بـ mp ففي هذه الحالة تنطق الـ p مثل:

تشنج cramp	معسكر camp
مصباح lamp	يثبت clamp
رطب/مبلل damp	منحدر ramp

(8) لا تنطق حرف p إذا بدأت الكلمة بـ ps مثل :

علم النفس psychology	الطب النفسي psychiatry
اسم مستعار pseudonym	محلل نفسي psychoanalyst
	مزمور/ ترنيمة psalm

(9) إذا كانت الكلمة تبدأ بـ pt فلا تنطق p مثل :

نقيع الشعير- شاي ptisan	مادة سامة ptomaine
قالب طي والتفاف الأوراق في البرعم ptyxis	منبت الريش pteryila
استرخاء جفن العين الأعلى ptosis	

(10) غالباً لا تنطق حرف الـ gh إذا وقعتا وسط الكلمة أو في نهايتها مثل :

من خلال through	bought

thorough شامل		fight يحارب	
high مرتفع		bright ساطع	
tight ضيق		thought تفكير	

(11) لا تنطق حرف r إذا جاء بعدها حرف ساكن أو إذا جاءت حرف آخر حرف في الكلمة، ولم يأت بعدها حرف متحرك مثل :

corn ذرة		corporation شركة	
turn دوران		harm أذى	
burn يحرق		writer كاتب	
alarm منبه		reader قارئ	
cord وتر		corner زاوية	
arm ذراع		cordiality مودة	
corpse جثة		fighter محارب	

(12) إذا انتهت الكلمة بـ gn أو gm فلا تنطق حرف g مثل :

sign ملامة	design تصميم
resign يستقبل	benign كريم
	paradigm صيغة

(13) إذا انتهت الكلمة بـ gue أو que فلا تنطق ue مثل :

catalogue كتالوج	tongue لسان
monologue مونولوج	league عصبة
vague غامض	plague وباء
unique وحيد- فريد	critique نقد

الحروف التي تنطق |ts| (تش) أو |s| (ش)

(14) انطق (ch) ، |ts| تش في أغلب الكلمات :

chew	يمضغ	cheap	رخيص
cheer	يهتف	chicory	الهندباء البرية
child	طفل	chief	رئيس/مدير
chips	رقائق	chance	فرصة
chat	دردشة	chest	صدر

(15) إذا وقع حرف t في منتصف الكلمة وتلاه حرف u أو i فينطقان |ts| تش أو |s| ش مثل:

nature	طبيعة	signature	توقيع
rapture	نشوة	feature	ملامح
nation	أمة	section	قسم
organization	منظمة	quotation	اقتباس

الحروف التي تنطق |s| (ش)

(16) انطق sh، |s| ش مثل :

sharp	حاد	shark	سمك القرش
shire	مقاطعة/ولاية	ship	سفينة
showman	مخرج المسرحية	showroom	صالة عرض
shrink	ينكمش	share	حصة
ash	رماد	shine	يلمع/يشرق

(17) إذا وقع الحرفان ss أو x في وسط الكلمة وتبعها حرف u أو i فانطق الحرفين |s| ش مثل:

pressure	ضغط	fissure	شق
passion	عاطفة	profession	مهنة
impression	انطباع	ss	mission	مهمة
aggression	عدوان	session	جلسة

X ⟶ anxious   sexual

(18) انطق sch ش |s| مثل:

نوع من الصخور schist   شحم-دهن schmaltz

حرف متحرك غير مشدد schwa

(19) انطق ci ش |s| مثل:

وجهي facial	خاص special
عنصري racial	اشتراكية socialism
اجتماعي social	الفاشية fascism

الحروف التى تنطق z

(20) ينطق حرف x فى الكلمة التى تبدأ بهذا الحرف z مثل :

xerography   xerox   الكريسماس xmas

(21) عندما يقع حرف s بين حرفين متحركين عادة ينطق z مثل :

سبب cause		واحة	oasis
تحليل analysis		زيارة	visit
خيانة treason		يزيد	raise
وقفة pause		مرحلة	phase
تصفيق applause		فصل	season
قاعدة base		يفقد	lose

(22) تنطق s الجمع z إذا سبقها صوت منطوق مثل:

مثل ، (b,g,v,z,m,I,r,j,w,g,a,e,I,o,u)

tables	hens
bags	tombs
rooms	cows
gabs	cars
computers	

(23) تنطق s الجمع |iz| إذا سبقها (s,z,sh,ch,g) :

boxes	watches
coaches	judges قضاة
bunches عناقيد	voices أصوات
dervishes دراويش	

الحروف التي تنطق ز أو ث أو جا

(24) إذا تلا حرف t حرف h فتكون المتتابع th فتنطق إما ث (خ) أو ز (ð) مثل:

(أ) انطقها ك ز /(ð) :

there	weather
feather ريش	father
those	this
others	

(ب) انطقها ك ث خ

ethnic عرقي	thin
thunder رعد	wrath غضب
thick كثيف	theater مسرح

(25) إذا وقع حرف s في وسط الكلمة وتبعها حرف u أو i فانطق الـ s جا **(ژ)** مثل:

pleasure سعادة	measure قياس
illusion خيال	conclusion خاتمة

| visual مرئي | seclusion عزلة |
| confusion ارتباك | |

نطق مختلف لبعض الحروف

(26) انطق الحرفين ph دائماً |f| مثل :

phenomenon ظاهرة	pharmacy
philosophy	elephant
pharynx بلعوم	telephone
phone	

(27) أحياناً ينطق حرف c على أنه |k| فى الحالات الآتية :

(أ) قبل الحرف الساكن ، وحرف a

clear	cloud سحابة
credit ائتمان	crime جريمة
cat	club
café	car

(ب) قبل حرف u

| cupid إله الحب | cure شفاء |
| culprit مجرم-مذنب | cumin كمون |

(ج) قبل حرف o

court محكمة	cow
covenant ميثاق	cover
courtship مغازلة	

وأحياناً أخرى ينطق على أنه s

(أ) قبل حرف e

| cell خلية | ceiling سقف |
| celebrate يحتفل | cellular خلوي |

cynic ساخر	cycle دورة
cyclone إعصار	cystitis التهاب المثانة

(ج) قبل حرف i

cinema	city
circumcision ختان	citadel قلعة
civil مدني	circumscribe يرسم خطًا حول

استثناءات : يمكن نطق c ش |s| إذا جاء بعدها حرف i مثل :

special خاص	facial
socialism اشتراكية	racial
fascism فاشية	social

(28) ed التى تضاف للفعل تنطق بعدة طرق

(أ) تنطق |t| إذا سبق ed ◄ (ch,sh,th,s,p,f,k) مثل :

helped	passed
washed	watched
baked	

(ب) تنطق |id| إذا سبق الـ ed ◄ t أو d مثل :

painted	patted
hated	faded

(ج) تنطق (d) فيما عدا السابق ذكره مثل :

played	allowed
closed	advised

(29) إذا تم إضافة s للجمع

(أ) تنطق |s| إذا سبقها صوت غير منطوق (s,f,p,k,th) مثل :

books	camps

roofs   أسقف   rats فئران

mouths أفواه

(ب) تنطق |z| إذا سبقها صوت منطوق (b,g,v,z,m,r,j,w,g,a,e,I,o,u) مثل :

tables طاولات   hens دجاج

bags   حقائب   tombs قبور

rooms   غرف   cows بقر

gabs   فجوات   cars سيارات

computers حواسيب

(ج) تنطق iz إذا سبقها (s,z,sh,ch,g) :

boxes   صناديق   watches ساعات

coaches مدربون   judges قضاة

bunches عناقيد   voices أصوات

dervishes دراويش

(30) تنطق الـ a فى الإنجليزية البريطانية a: أما فى الإنجليزية الأمريكية فتنطق ae مثل :

Brit. Eng.	glass /	gla:s/	Am. Eng.	class /	Klae/
	farm /	fa: m /		pass /	paes/

(31) يمكن نطق sch فى بداية الكلمة بثلاث طرق

(أ) ينطق (sk) مثل:

school   scholar مثقف

scholastic دراسي   scheme مخطط

(ب) ينطق /s/ مثل :

schmaltz شحم   schist صخر

schwa حرف على بلا نغمة

(ج) ينطق /s/ مثل :

schismatic انشقاقي   schism انشقاق

(32) الكلمات التي تنتهي بـ ary, ory, ery تنطق في الإنجليزية الأمريكية بإظهار الحرف المتحرك ، وفي الإنجليزية البريطانية بإخفاء الحرف المتحرك مثل:

dictionary	obligatory
stationary	ordinary
laboratory	repository مخزن/مستودع

(33) إذا وقع حرف L قبل حرف متحرك أو حرفين فتسمى L واضحة (clear L) مثل :

letter خطاب	light ضوء
let يسمح	look نظرة
labour عمل	lorry شاحنة
leek كرات	

أما إذا وقعت في نهاية الكلمة فتسمى مظلمة (dark L) مثل :

result نتيجة	consult يستشير
kill يقتل	fill يملأ
mill طاحونة	

ENGLICH WITHOUT MICTAKES

Word Formation
تكوين الكلمة

Chapter 3

تتكون العديد من الكلمات فى اللغة الإنجليزية بإضافة بادئة إلى بداية الكلمة أو لاحقة إلى نهاية الكلمة ، وهذه الملحقات لا تستخدم منفردة ، ولكنها تلحق بأجزاء الكلمة ، ويطلق عليها بادئة prefix عندما تأتى ببداية الكلمة ، كما يطلق عليها لاحقة suffix عندما تأتى فى نهاية الكلمة، ويضيف prefix معنى جديداً إلى الكلمة الأصلية، ولكن suffix يغير من مشتقات الكلمة ، وهذه تعد إحدى الصعوبات المهمة التى تواجه العديد من الطلبة فى المراحل التعليمية المختلفة. وهناك أسئلة متكررة من الطلبة حول هذه الكلمات، وعلى سبيل المثال لا الحصر قد يتبادر إلى ذهن الطالب سؤال لماذا كلمة illegal عكس كلمة legal وليست dislegal أو unlegal، وبالقطع فإن شكوى الطالب قد تكون فى محلها للوهلة الأولى، وبما أننا لسنا بصدد دراسة تاريخ اللغة فإننا يجب أن نعرف التعبيرات كما وصلتنا ومع كل هذا فإن هناك بعض القواعد قد يكون لها دورها وفائدتها لكل الطلبة والدارسين عبر المراحل التعليمية المختلفة وهى كالآتى:

(1) الكلمات التى تنتهى بـ ify هى أفعال .

يثقف edify		يصنف classify
يجمل beautify		يدون codify
يميز identify		يبسط simplify

(2) الكلمات التى تنتهى بـ ise أو ize هى أفعال .

يهذب civilise	يقتصد economise
ينظم organise	ينقد criticise
يستقطب polarize	يعظم-يزيد maximise
يضبط regularize	يدخل المستشفى hospitalize
	ينشر popularize

تحويل الأفعال إلى أسماء

(3) أضف ion إلى غالبية الأفعال التى تنتهى بـ ss عند تحويلها إلى أسماء .

يعبر express	expression
يعلق obsess	obsession
يحزن depress	depression
يعترف confess	confession
يقمع suppress	suppression

(4) عند تحويل الأفعال التى تنتهى بـ ct إلى أسماء أضف ion إلى نهاية الفعل .

يتنبأ predict	prediction
يتواصل connect	connection
يعكس reflect	reflection
يجذب attract	attraction

expect يتوقع　　　　　　　　　　expectation

(5) عند تحويل الأفعال التى تنتهى بـ it إلى أسماء أضف ion إلى نهاية الفعل .

prohibit يحظر　　　　　　　　　prohibition

inhibit يثبط　　　　　　　　　　inhibition

exhibit يعرض　　　　　　　　　exhibition

(6) عند تحويل الأفعال التى تنتهى بـ ate إلى أسماء احذف حرف e وضع ion

operate يشغل　　　　　　　　　operation

hesitate يتردد　　　　　　　　　hesitation

irrigate يروي　　　　　　　　　irrigation

meditate يتأمل　　　　meditation

irritate يثير　　　　　　　　　irritation

(7) عند تحويل الأفعال التى تنتهى بـ pt إلى أسماء أضف ion إلى نهاية الفعل .

corrupt يفسد　　　　　　　　　corruption

disrupt يخل　　　　　　　　　disruption

(8) عند تحويل الأفعال التى تنتهى بـ ise أو ize احذف حرف e وأضف ation إلى نهاية الفعل

civilise يهذب　　　　　　　　civilisation

organize ينظم　　　　　　　　organization

realize يدرك　　　　　　　　realization

humanize يضفي عليه صفة الإنسانية　　　　　humanization

criticize ينقد　　　　　criticism

recognize يتعرف على　　　recognition

(9) لاشتقاق الاسم من الأفعال السابقة والتى تنتهى بـ ify تحول الـ y إلى i ثم تضاف cation .

classify يصنف	classification
edify يثقف	edification
identify يميز	identification
beautify يجمل	beautification

(10) معظم الأفعال ذات المد القصير والتى تنتهى بـ ve عند تحويلها إلى أسماء يتم تغيير ve إلى ution

evolve يطور	evolution
solve يحل	solution
absolve يتحرر من	absolution
revolve يتمحور	revolution

استثناءات:

| involve يشمل | involvement |

(11) عند تحويل الأفعال التى تنتهى بـ ute إلى أسماء نستبدل ute بـ ution

attribute ينعت	attribution
contribute يساهم	contribution
distribute يوزع	distribution
substitute بديل	substitution

(12) عند تحويل الأفعال التى تنتهى بـ be إلى أسماء استبدل be بـ ption

describe يصف	description
prescribe يصف علاجًا	prescription
subscribe يشترك	subscription
inscribe ينقش	inscription

(13) عند تحويل معظم الأفعال التى تنتهى بـ me إلى أسماء احذف e وأضف ption

consume يستهلك	consumption
presume يفترض	presumption
resume يستأنف	resumption

(14) عند تحويل معظم الأفعال التى تنتهى بـ eive إلى أسماء احذف eive وأضف eption

conceive يفكر	conception
deceive يخدع	deception
receive يتسلم	reception
perceive يدرك	perception

(15) عند تحويل الأفعال التى تنتهى بـ el إلى أسماء نستبدل el بـ ulsion

propel يحث	propulsion
expel يقذف	expulsion
compel يجبر	compulsion
repel يعارض	repulsion

استثناءات:

rebel	rebellion

(16) عند تحويل معظم الأفعال التى تنتهى بـ de إلى أسماء احذف de وأضف sion

evade يتهرب	evasion
include يتضمن	inclusion
conclude ينهي	conclusion
explode يفجر	explosion

استثناءات:

(17) غالبية الأفعال ذات المد والتى تنتهى بـ ve عند تحويلها إلى اسم نستبدل ve بـ f

believe	يعتقد	belief
grieve	يحزن	grief
relieve	يعفي	relief
prove	يبرهن	proof

استثناءات:

(18) للحصول على صيغة الفاعل من الفعل أضف r أو er إلى نهاية الفعل .

believe	يعتقد	believer
erase	يحذف	eraser
love	يحب	lover
lose	يفقد	loser
come	يأتي	comer
read	يقرأ	reader
play	يلعب	player
think	يفكر	thinker
keep	يحفظ	keeper
lend	يقرض	lender

(19) الأفعال التى تنتهى بـ t أو ss تأخذ or

invent	يخترع	inventor
confess	يعترف	confessor
visit	يزور	visitor
compress	يضغط	compressor

(20) بعض الكلمات تأخذ ist لاشتقاق صيغة الفاعل منها .

type	يطبع	typist طابع
piano	آلة البيانو	pianist عازف بيانو
art	فن	artist فنان

تحويل الاسم إلى صفة

(1) عندما يضاف إلى نهاية الكلمة (suffix) النهايات التالية فهى اسم .

ment ⟶ agreement اتفاق, settlement تسوية

ness ⟶ happiness سعادة, sadness حزن

dom ⟶ kingdom مملكة, wisdom حكمة

acy ⟶ accuracy ذمة, theocracy سلطة دينية

ure ⟶ pleasure سعادة, closure إغلاق

ism ⟶ realism واقعية, criticism نقد

ity ⟶ formality شكليات, complexity تعقيد, curiosity فضول

cs ⟶ economics علم الاقتصاد, politics علم السياسة

ssion ⟶ expression تعبير, possession ملكية

sion ⟶ vision رؤية

al ⟶ arrival وصول

hood ⟶ childhood طفولة, motherhood أمومة

cation ⟶ identification هوية, communication اتصال

tion ⟶ immigration هجرة , civilization حضارة

ship ⟶ friendship صداقة, citizenship مواطنة

age ⟶ hostage رهنية, postage رسوم البريد

th ⟶ truth حقيقة, growth نمو

ance ⟶ distance مسافة, importance أهمية

ture ⟶ creature مخلوق, feature ملامح

our ⟶ humour فكاهة, favour معروف

(2) يضاف المقطع less إلى الأسماء لتحويلها إلى صفات (ذات معنى عكسى).

careless مهمل   hopeless

thoughtless أرعن   treeless

childless بلا ولد   homeless

(3) أضف اللاحقة ic لتحويل الاسم إلى الصفة مع إلغاء حرف e أو y فى بعض الحالات.

atom ذرة   atomic

athlete رياضى   athletic

economy اقتصاد   economic

history تاريخ   historic

(4) أضف اللاحقة tic إلى الأسماء التى تنتهى بـ ma لتحويلها إلى صفة.

drama دراما   dramatic

aroma رائحة   aromatic

dogma مذهب   dogmatic

charisma جاذبية   charismatic

(5) أضف اللاحقة atic إلى الأسماء التى تنتهى بحرف m لتحويلها إلى صفة .

idiom اصطلاح   idiomatic

axiom قاعدة بديهية   axiomatic

system نظام   systematic

(6) أضف اللاحقة al لتغيير الأسماء إلى صفات ، وفى بعض الأحيان يستوجب هذا حذف e أو y من نهاية الاسم وإضافة ial بدلاً من e أو y .

herb أعشاب	herbal
center مركز	central
industy صناعة	industrial

(7) أضف اللاحقة al إلى معظم الأسماء ذات الأصل اللاتينى والتى تنتهى بـ ic أو ics (بعد حذف s) عند التحويل إلى صفة.

music موسيقى	musical
logic منطق	logical
ethics أخلاقيات	ethical
mathematics رياضيات	mathematical

(8) هناك العديد من الصفات التى تنتهى بـ al وليس لها اسم .

legal قانونى	vital
oral شفهى	dental
final نهائى	rural

(9) أضف اللاحقة ial إلى بعض الأسماء عند تحويلها من اسم إلى صفة.

commerce تجارة	commercial
province إقليم	provincial
president رئيس	presidential
confidence ثقة	confidential

(10) أضف اللاحقة ual عند تحويل بعض الأسماء إلى صفات .

text نص	textual
habit عادة	habitual
context سياق	contextual
sex جنس	sexual

(11) أضف ar إلى الأسماء التى تنتهى بـ cle ، gle ، ule عند تحويلها إلى صفة

دائرة circle	circular
angle زاوية	angular
muscle عضلية	muscular
molecule جزيء	molecular

(12) هناك بعض الصفات تنتهى بـ ar وليس لها اسم .

شمسي solar	lunar قمري
insular جزيري	stellar نجمي

(13) بعض الصفات تنتهى بـ ic - al - ar تستخدم كاسم

final نهائي	natural طبيعي
commercial تجاري	academic أكاديمي

(14) قد يشتق من بعض الأسماء صفتان أحدهما تنتهى بـ ic والأخرى تنتهى بـ cal وفى مثل هذه الحالات يجب البحث عن الكلمة في القاموس لمعرفة التباين فى المعنى .

economic اقتصادي	economical
historic تاريخي	historical

(15) نضيف er أو ese أو an إلى أسماء الأماكن ، لتوضيح أن شخصا ينتمى إلى هذا المكان .

Londoner	New Yorker
Icelander	New Zealander
Chinese	Japanese
Sudanese	Portuguese
American	Italian

African   Indian

(16) ملحوظة : اللاحقة ese تستخدم للإشارة إلى لغة مكان معين أو شعب معين .

Burmese   Chinese   Japanese

(17) عند تحويل الصفات التى تنتهى بـ nt إلى أسماء استبدل t بـ ce أو cy .

different مختلف   difference

distant بعيد   distance

reluctant ممانع   reluctance

obedient مطيع   obedience

constant مستمر   constancy

efficient كفء   efficiency

sufficient كافٍ   sufficiency

تحويل الصفات إلى عكسها

(1) الغالبية العظمى من الكلمات التى تنتهى بـ able أو ible هى صفات.

agreeable مقبول   possible

readable مقروء   horrible

desirable مرغوب فيه

لتحويل الصفة إلى عكسها اتبع التالى :

(2) الصفات التى تبدأ بحرف m :

يضاف im إلى بداية الصفة

moral أخلاقي   immoral

mobile متحرك   immobile

immortal   بشري mortal

immature   ناضج mature

(3) الصفات التى تبدأ بحرف L :

يضاف il إلى بداية الصفة

illegal   قانوني legal

illegitimate   شرعي legitimate

illogical   منطقي logical

illiterate   متعلم literate

(4) الصفات التى تبدأ بحرف r :

يضاف ir إلى بداية الصفة

irregular   منتظم regular

irrelevant   متصل relevant

irrational   معقول rational

irreligious   متدين religious

(5) الصفات التى تبدأ بحرف p :

يضاف im إلى بداية الصفة .

impossible   محتمل possible

impolite   مؤدب polite

impersonal   شخصي personal

(6) عادة ما تضاف البادئة un إلى الصفات التى تنتهى بـ able فى حين أن البادئة in تضاف إلى الصفات التى تنتهى بـ ible عند التحويل إلى صيغة النفى .

غير مصدق unbelievable   غير مقبول unacceptable

غير مصدق incredible   خفي invisible

inconceivable غير معقول   inadvisable

(7) لاحظ أن البادئة un أحياناً تعنى (ليس حسنا بشكل كاف) ، وأن السابقة non تعنى (ليس له علاقة

بـ) .

unmusical   ليس موسيقيًا بقدر كاف

non-musical   لا علاقة له بالموسيقى

uneconomic   ليس اقتصاديًا بقدر كاف

non-economic   لا علاقة له بالاقتصاد

(8) البادئة anti تضاف إلى الصفة لتعنى (ضد) :

antifeminist   antiwar

antislavery   antisocial

(9) معظم الكلمات التى تنتهى بـ ly هى ظروف .

accurately   quickly

slowly   cleverly

lovely   ugly

fatherly   brotherly

sisterly   motherly

(10) ملحوظة : بعض الصفات التى تشير إلى الجنسية تعد شاذة .

Greece   Greek

Wales   welsh

Holland   Dutch

Switzerland   Swiss

تحويل الأسماء والصفات إلى أفعال

(1) أضف اللاحقة en لتحويل الصفات ذات المقطع الواحد إلى أفعال .

black	blacken
white	whiten
red	redden
hard	harden

استثناءات : القاعدة لا تنطبق على الصفات التى تنتهى بـ th-r-l-ng-n

young	green
thin	worth مستحق
cruel قاس	

(2) أضف اللاحقة ify لتحويل الصفات أو الأسماء ذات المقطع الواحد إلى أفعال .

class	classify
code	codify
pure	purify
simple	simplify

(3) أضف اللاحقة ise - أو ize - لتحويل الأسماء والصفات ذات الأصل اللاتينى أو اليونانى من مقطعين أو أكثر إلى أفعال .

liquid سائل	liquidise
summary موجز	summarise
legal	legalise
popular	popularise

(1) تحويل الكلمة إلى عكسها :

لتحويل الكلمة إلى عكسها أضف في مقدمة الكلمة mis-,dis-,in-,un

uncooked	unhappy
insecure	inaccurate
non-academic	non-human
misuse	misinterpret
disconnect	disappear

(2) للمرة الثانية أو بطريقة مختلفة :

أضف البادئة re إلى الكلمات لكي تعني إما إعادة الفعل (للمرة الثانية) أو (بطريقة مختلفة).

re-arrange	re-write
re-elect	re-appear

(3) قبل أو بعد :

أضف البادئة pre وتعني (قبل) والبادئة post وتعني (بعد) لاشتقاق فرق طفيف في المعنى .

pre-war	pre-school
post-modemism	post-graduate

(4) قليل جداً أو كثير جداً :

تضاف البادئة under لتعني (قليل جداً) ، والبادئة over لتعني (كثير جداً) .

يبخس القيمة underestimate	دون الاستخدام underused
يتحمل underage	متخلف underdeveloped
سوء تغذية underfed	يبخس underrate
over-generalize يعمم	يجهد نفسه بالعمل overwork
يمثل بشكل مبالغ فيه overact	

(5) الصغر أو التحبب :

تشير بعض اللواحق بنهاية الكلمة إلى صفة الصغر أو التحبب :

مثل y , i , ie

عمتي Auntie   بيتي betty

عزيز Sweetie   ماكر wily

أو مثل ette

منديل ورقي رطب towelette   حجرة طعام صغيرة dinette

أو مثل ling

صبية darling   بطة صغيرة duckling

أو مثل t

دائرة صغيرة circlet

أو مثل let

كتيب booklet   نجم صاعد starlet

ENGLISH
WITHOUT
MISTAKES

الكلمات المركبة والاختصارات

(1) تركيب مزجى (blends): بعض الكلمات تتكون من كلمتين يطلق عليهما باللغة العربية (تركيب مزجى) وعند تحويل الكلمتين إلى هذا التركيب يستخدم فقط أجزاء من الكلمتين، ويستخدم الصحفيون والمعلنون الكثير من هذه الكلمات بهذه الطريقة ، وإليك البعض منها والتى تعتبر جزءًا من المفردات العامة للغة .

agriculture زراعة + business	agribusiness أعمال زراعية
elector + execution	electrocution صعق كهربائى
helicopter + airport	heliport مهبط الطائرة العمودية
motor + hotel	motel فندق على الطريق العام
news + broad cast	newscast نشرة الأخبار
smoke + fog	smog ضباب دخانى
stagnation + inflation	stagflation ركود تضخمى
television + marathon	telethon حفل خيري
transfer + resistor	transistor مذياع صغير

(2) Acronyms (حروف كلمة مؤلفة من عدة كلمات أخرى)

وهى تتكون من الحروف الأولى لمجموعة من الكلمات، وهى غالباً ما تكتب بحروف كبيرة بدون نقاط بينها وتنطق على أنها كلمات، والقليل من هذه الحروف المكونة لمجموعة كلمات أصبح شائع الاستخدام، خصوصاً بالنسبة للكلمات التى تتصل بالعلم.

LASER	Lightware Amplification by Simulated Emission of Radiation
	الليزر (تضخيم الضوء بانبعاث الإشعاع المحفز).
RADAR	Radio Detection and Rejection
	رادار (نظام استخدام الموجات للتعرف على الأجسام الثابتة والمتحركة).
SONAR	Sound Navigation Ranging نظام كشف الصوت
LORAN	Lont Range Navigation نظام الكشف طويل المدى
NATO	North Atlantic Treaty Organization
	منظمة حلف شمال الأطلنطي
UNIDO	United Nations Industerial Development Organizationمنظمة
	الأمم المتحدة للتنمية الصناعية
FAO	Food and Agriculture Organization
	منظمة الأغذية والزراعة
UNICEF	صندوق الأمم المتحدة United Nations International Children's Fund
	للطفولة
ICAO	International Civil Aviation Organization
	المنظمة الدولية للطيران المدني
INGOs	المنظمات الدولية International NonGovernmental organizations
	غير الحكومية

(3) two - word verbs (أفعال ذات كلمتين)

الكثير من الأفعال ذات الكلمتين تصبح أسماء ، وقد تكتب هذه الأسماء بدون أية فاصلة أو بفاصلة بين الكلمتين ومعظم هذه الكلمات هى لغة عامية ، لا تستخدم فى الكتابة الرسمية وهى ذات معنى متغير ، وهى عرف هذا النوع بين جماعات معينة .

الكلمة	الكلمة المركبة
blow	ثقب فى إطار السيارة blow out

الكلمة	الكلمة المركبة
blow	تكبير لصورة blow - up
build	تحضير إعلامى - تزايد buildup
call	يطلب بالتليفون call-up
cut	تخفيض فى الإنتاج cutback
cut	حد - مستقطع - حدود cutoff
pay	دفع الرواتب أو payoff
	ذروة - عقاب - الأرباح
run	مرهق - متهدم run-down
	مشاجرة run-in
run	الدورة الحاسمة run-off
show	تباهى - تفاخر show-off
show	حسم لنزاع أو قضية - المكاشفة showdown

ملحوظة (أ) هناك أسماء قليلة تتكون من الفعل فى وضع النهاية أى بعد الجزء الأول مثل:

فتحة شفط intake		مدخلات	input
محصلة outcome		اندلاع	outbreak
الناتج output		منفذ	outlet
تربية upbringing		امتداد	out reach
		صيانة	upkeep

ملحوظة (ب) هناك أفعال قليلة يكتب بها الفعل الأساسى بالموضع الأخير مثل :

overlook يتجاهل   overdo يفرط

uphold يحافظ على   overturn يبطل

(4) ملحقات أول الكلمة (prefixes) :

الملحقات بأول الكلمة هى عبارة عن إضافات من مقطع أو مقطعين فى بداية الكلمة، والتى تغير من معناها ولكن لا تغير مشتقات الكلمة ، فإذا كانت الكلمة اسمًا تبقى اسما كما هى وإذا كانت صفة تبقى صفة كما هى وهكذا ، ومن الجدير بالملاحظة أن الملحقات لا يتبعها حاليا أية فاصلة، وإذا كان هناك شك فى ذلك فما عليك إلا البحث عن الكلمة فى القاموس، وبالإضافة إلى كل هذا، هناك عدد كبير جداً من الملحقات فى مقدمات الكلمات تشير إلى النواحى السلبية مثل non, in, dis, counter, a وقد يكون لنفس الكلمة أكثر من معنى عند إضافة أكثر من لاحقة بأولها ، لاحظ الإشارة إلى هذه الكلمات من خلال أدوات مثل a, an, the للأسماء التى لا تعد .

PREFIX	MEANING	EXAMPLE
a	not	amoral لا أخلاقي
ante	before	antedate يؤرخ بتاريخ سابق
anti	against	antifreeze مادة مقاومة للتجميد
arch	highest	archbishop مطران
auto	self	autobiography سيرة ذاتية

PREFIX	MEANING	EXAMPLE
bi	two	bicycle دراجة
		bisect يشطر
co	with	bicentennial مائتي سنة
		coordinate ينسق
		copilot مساعد طيار
counter	against عكس	counter clockwise عكس عقارب الساعة
	opposite to مضاد	counter revolution ثورة مضادة
de	reverse action	defrost يذيب
dis	not	disloyal خائن
	reverse action	disconnect انقطاع الاتصال
ex	former	ex-president رئيس سابق
	out of	expatriate مغترب

PREFIX	MEANING	EXAMPLE
exo	outside	exo-skeleton
fore	before	foretell تنبأ
hyper	too much	hypersensitive مفرط الحساسية
in-il-im-ir	not	insensitive متبلد الشعور
inter	between - among	international دولي
mal	bad - badly	malformed مشوه
maxi	most, large	maxiskirt تنورة طويلة
mini	least, small	miniskirt تنورة قصيرة
mis	wrong, wrongly	misprint خطأ مطبعي
mono	one	monorail خط حديدي أحادي السكة
multi	many	multiracial متعدد الأعراق
neo	new, revived	neocolonialism الاستعمار الجديد

PREFIX	MEANING	EXAMPLE
non	not, without	nonstop دون توقف
out	to do something to a greater degree	to outdo يتغلب
	away from	
	Too much	outpatient عيادة خارجية
Over	Above	to overeat يلتهم
	alongside	overpass اجتاز
para	after	paraphrase يعيد صياغة
post	before	postwar بعد الحرب
pre	on the side of, in favor of	prewar قبل الحرب
pro	first, original,	pro-communist موال للشيوعية
	false, imitation	
proto	four	prototype نموذج
pseudo	again, renew	pseudo-classic شبه الكلاسيك

PREFIX	MEANING	EXAMPLE
quad	half, partly	quadrangle رباعي الزوايا
re		to restart يعيد تشغيل
semi	beneath, less, lower than	semiprivate شبه خاص
		semicircle نصف دائرة
sub	from one place to another, across	subway نفق
		subnormal متخلف عقليًا
trans	from one place to another, across	to transport
		transatlantic عابر للأطلسي
tri	three	tricycle دراجة ثلاثية العجلات

* * *

هى عبارة عن نهايات تضاف إلى الكلمة ، وتغير من اشتقاق الكلمة ، وقد تغير من معناها أيضاً ، وقد يضاف للكلمة الواحدة أكثر من لاحقة في نهايتها، كما أود الإشارة إلى أن الملحقات s,-ed- في نهاية الأفعال العادية والملحقات es,s في نهاية الأسماء الجمع لا تغير اشتقاق الكلمة ، أى بمعنى أن الكلمة تبقى كما هى ، فإذا كانت فعلاً تظل فعلاً وإذا كانت اسما تظل كما هى أيضاً .

SUFFIX	MEANING	EXAMPLE
able, ible	able to be , having the quality of	teach يعلم teachable قابل للتعلم reduce يقلل reducible قليل
al	having the quality of, related to	nation وطن national وطني person شخص personal شخصي
ant	having the quality to	tolerate يتسامح tolerant متسامح dominate يسود dominant سائد
arian	having the quality of	authority سلطة authoritarian سلطوي
ative	connected with	argument جدال argumentative جدلي

SUFFIX	MEANING	EXAMPLE
ed	adjective from nouns and verbs	جدار wall محاط بجدار walled please يسعد pleased سعيد
ese	showing national origin	Lebanon لبنان Lebanese لبناني China الصين Chinese صيني
esque	in the style of	picture صورة picturesque تصويري Roman روماني Romanesque طراز روماني
ic	having the quality of	democracy ديمقراطية democratic ديمقراطي
ical	having the quality of	theory نظرية theoretical نظري
ish	belonging to (national origin)	Swede السويد Swedish سويدي
ish	somewhat, approximately	young صغير youngish صغير بعض الشيء

SUFFIX	MEANING	EXAMPLE
ive	having the quality of	explode ينفجر explosive مادة متفجرة collect يجمع collective جماعي
less	without, lacking in	child طفل childless بلا أطفال
like	having the quality of	child طفل childlike طفولي
ous, eous, ious	having the quality of	virtue فضيلة virtuous فاضل courtesy لطف courteous لطيف ambition طُموح ambitious طَموح
some	full of	burden يثقل burdensome مرهق bother يزعج bothersome مزعج
worthy	deserving	praise يمدح praisworthy جدير بالثناء

SUFFIX	MEANING	EXAMPLE
y	full of, covered with, having the quality of	hair شعر hairy مشعر sand رمل sandy رملي brain عقل brainy ذكي
ful	having the quality of	meaning مغزى meaningful ذو مغزى thank يشكر thankful شاكر

***

(5) هذه الملحقات تشير إلى الناس ، وهي تحول الكلمات من صيغتها إلى أسماء:

SUFFIX	MEANING	EXAMPLE
an	member of, belonging to, favoring	Atlanta أتلانتا Atlantan أتلانتي republic جمهورية republican جمهوري
ant,ent	agent, a person who does, makes	inhabit يسكن inhabitant ساكن correspond يراسل correspondent مراسل
arian	belonging to a group, favoring	vegetables خضراوات vegetarian نباتي authority سلطة authoritarian سلطوي
crat	a person connected with	democracy ديمقراطية democrat ديمقراطي bureaucracy بيروقراطية bureaucrat بيروقراطي
ee	variation of-er, a person	absent غائب absentee متغيب employ يوظف employee موظف

SUFFIX	MEANING	EXAMPLE
eer	a person who does, operates	auction مزاد auctioneer دلال engine محرك engineer مهندس
er	a person who does, makes	back يخبز baker خباز dream يحلم dreamer حالم
ese	national origin	Portugal البرتغال Portuguese برتغالي China الصين Chinese صيني
ette	feminine form	usher حاجب usherette حاجبة
ian	connected with	Paris باريس Parisian باريسي
ite	member of group	social اجتماعي socialite عضو بارز في المجتمع
let	small, unimportant	star نجم starlet ممثلة ناشئة
ling	unimportant (derogatory)	weak ضعيف weakling ضعيف الجسم
or	variation of-er, a person who...	survive يحيا- ينجو من survivor ناج

SUFFIX	MEANING	EXAMPLE
ster	a person making or doing something a member of	trick يخدع trickster مخادع gang عصابة gangster عضو في عصابة
y	familiar form (usually used in family, with children)	dad, daddy bill , billy

(6) ملحقات تشير إلى الأشياء

Suffix	Meaning	Example
age	extent, amount	drain يصرف draingage مصرف sink ينخفض sinkage منخفض
ant	agent, personal or impersonal : the thing that... the person who	lubricate يشحمlubricant مادة التشحيم inform يخبر informant مخبر

Suffix	Meaning	Example
ation, ition	institution, condition of being done	organize ينظم organization منظمة educate يعلم education تعليم nourish يغذي nutrition غذاء note يدون notation تدوين
er	agent, the thin that... something having	silence صمت silencer كاتم الصوت two wheels, two wheeler
ery	place of activity	refine يصفي refinery مصفاة surgeon جراح surgery جراحة
ery	collective, uncountable	machine ماكينة machinery ماكينات baskets سلال basketry على شكل سلة

Suffix	Meaning	Example
ette	small, compact	kitchen مطبخ kitchenette مطبخ صغير room غرفة roomette غرفة صغيرة leather جلد leatherette جلدي
ful	the amount contained	mouth فم mouthful ملء الفم - cup كوب cupful ملء كوب
ing	turns countable nouns into uncountable indicating material	pipe أنبوب piping مجموعة أنابيب wire سلك wiring شبكة أسلاك panel هيئة محلفين paneling تشكيل هيئة محلفين walk يمشي walking مشى
let	small, unimportant	pig خنزير piglet خنزير صغير

Suffix	Meaning	Example
or	thing that...	conduct يوصِّل conductor موصِّل
y (sometimes-ie)	familiar	nightgown ثوب nighty قميص النوم dog كلب doggy كلب صغير bird طائر birdie طائر صغير

(7) الأسماء المجردة:

Suffix	Meaning	Example
age	act of , extent	marry يتزوج marriage زواج cover يغطي coverage تغطية shrink ينكمش shrinkage انكماش
ance, ence	activity, condition	guide مرشد guidance إرشاد attend حضر attendant حاضر independent مستقل independence استقلال

Suffix	Meaning	Example
ancy, ency	activity, condition of being	constant مستمر constancy استمرارية
ation	state of doing something	dominate يسيطر domination سيطرة communicate يتصل communication اتصال
ery	domain, condition	brave شجاع bravery شجاعة slave عبد slavery عبودية
hood	status	false زائف falsehood زيف mother أم motherhood أمومة
ion	act of doing something	confession يعترفconfess اعتراف
ism	doctrine, belief, condition	communism شيوعية absenteeism organism نظام غياب

Suffix	Meaning	Example
ity	state, quality	complex معقد complexity تعقيد curious فضول curiosity فضولي sane عاقل sanity سلامة العقل
ment	state, action	arrange يرتبarrangement ترتيب govern يحكمgovernment حكومة
ness	state, condition	ill مريض illness مرض selfish أناني selfishness أنانية
ocray	system of government organization	democrat ديمقراطي democracy ديمقراطية autocrat حاكم مطلق autocracy حكم مطلق
ship	status, condition	friend صديق friendship صداقة hard صلب hardship صلابة

Suffix	Meaning	Example
ly (ally after ic and ment)	in the manner of	strange غريب strangely بغرابة happy سعيد happily بسعادة comic كوميدي comically بطريقة كوميدية basic أساسي basically بشكل أساسي fundamental
ward	manner, direction of movement	home منزل homeward on , تجاه المنزل onward/ after afterward/ back backward
wise	in the manner	clock, clockwise
ate	cause to become	regular, regulate active, activate
en	cause to become	tight, tighten deaf, deafen
ify	cause to become	beauty , beautify simple , simplify

Suffix	Meaning	Example
ize	cause to become	شعبي popular ينشر popularize مستشفى hospital يدخل المستشفى hospitalize منظم regular ينظم regularize

(9) أصول اشتقاق الكلمات roots

باستطاعتك زيادة حصيلتك من الكلمات الإنجليزية من خلال تعلم أصول اشتقاق الكلمات ذات الأصل اللاتيني أو اليوناني ، فما يقرب من أكثر من نصف الكلمات الإنجليزية ذات أصل لاتيني أو يوناني ، والقائمة التالية لهذا التوضيح شائعة من السهل رؤيتها في الكلمات الإنجليزية ، وهي مميزة بحرف i الكبير للإشارة إلى اللاتينية وحرف g الكبير للإشارة إلى اليونانية ، ومن الجدير بالملاحظة أن معظم المصطلحات العلمية ذات أصل يوناني أما معظم المصطلحات الأدبية ذات أصل لاتيني والقليل منها ذات أصل إنجليزي ، وبدون أية ملحقات في بداية أو نهاية الكلمات .

Root	MEANING	English Words
alien	another, foreign	inalienable يبعد alienate قابل للتحول alienation أبعاد
am	love	amiable ودود amity وئام amicable حبي
anim	mind, life	animal حيوان animate جعله حيويًا animism مذهب حيوية المادة
anthrop	human being	anthropology علم الإنسان anthropomorphic مجسم misanthrope عدو الإنسان

Root	MEANING	English Words
arch	rule, chief	anarchy فوضىmonarchy ملكيةarchitect مهندس معماري
aud	hear	audio سمعي auditorium هالة كبيرة audible مسموع
auto	self	automobile سيارة automatic ذاتي الحركة autobiography سيرة ذاتية
bene	good, well	beneficial مفيد benefactor benevolent متبرعخيِّر
bio	life	biology علم الأحياءbiosphere المحيط الحيوي biography سيرة ذاتية
caust	burn	caustic مادة كاوية cauterize عالج بالكي holocaust محرقة
cent	hundred	century قرنcentipede أم أربع وأربعين centigrade مئوي

Root	MEANING	English Words
chron	time	chronologyمزمنchronic تسلسل زمني anachronism مفارقة تاريخية
cide	kill	insecticide انتحارsuicide مبيد حشرات genocide إبادة جماعية
cosm	order, world	كوني cosmic تجميلي cosmetic cosmopolitan عالمي
cred	believe	ائتمان credit عقيدة creed discredit عدم الثقة
crit	judge	ناقد critic معيار criterion criticism نقد
dem	people	democracy ديمقراطية epidemic وباءendemic مرض متوطن

Root	MEANING	English Words
derm	skin	dermatitis التهاب الجلد dermatology طب الأمراض الجلدية epidermis بشرة
domin	master, lord	dominion سيادةdominate يسودpredominate يهيمن
dynam	power, force	dynamic حيوي dynamo دينامو dynamite ديناميت
fac	make	factory مصنعmanufacture facsimile فاكسيصنع
fin	end, limit	finish ينهي finite محدود define يحدد
fort	strong	fortress قلعة fortify يحصن effort جهد
frat	brother	fraternity أخوةfraternal fraternize يتآخىأخوي
geo	earth	geography جغرافياgeology جيولوجيا geode حجر كريم

Root	MEANING	English Words
graph	write	monographic بياني graphic دراسي مقتضب demography علم السكان
hydra	water	hydraulic صنبور hydrant هيدروليكي dehydrate يجفف
litera	letter	illiterate أمي literature أدب literal حرفي
log	word, science of	علم الأحياء biology astrology علم التنجيم physiology علم وظائف الأعضاء
magn	great	magnate قطب magnify يكبر magnanimous شهم
manu	hand	manuscript دليل manual مخطوط manus اليد
mater	mother	matron رئيسة الممرضات maternity أمومي maternal أمومة

Root	MEANING	English Words
meter	measure	kilometer كيلومتر thermometer مقياس الحرارة metric متري
micro	small	microscope ميكروسكوب microbe, ميكروب microcosm عالم صغير
multi	much, many	multiply يضاعفmultitude تعددmultiform متعدد الأشكال
mon	alone	monopoly احتكارlmonotone أحادي النغم
mut	change	mutant متحول commute ينتقلimmutable ثابت
neo	new	neonatal حديثي الولادة neoclassical كلاسيكية جديدة neocolonialism الاستعمار الجديد

Root	MEANING	English Words
nom	law	astronomy علم الفلك الاقتصادي economy
nomin- nomen	name	Nominate يرشح
nym	name	pseudonym مستعار
op,oper	work	operate يشغلinoperable متعذر التطبيق
pan	all, whole	panorama بانوراما
pater	father	paternal أبوي
path	feeling	pathetic مثير للشفقة
ped	child	pediatric ذو علاقة بطب الأطفال
ped	foot	
phil	love	philosophy فلسفة
phys	body,nature	physical بدني
phon	sound, voice	telephone
phos,phot	light	photograph
plen	full	plenty وفرة
poli	city	politics علم السياسة
port	carry	export يصدر
prim	first, original	primitive بدائي
psych	soul	psychology علم النفس
rup	break	Interrupt يقاطع
scop,	book at	microscope ميكروسكوب
scrib, script	write	script سيناريو describe يصف

Root	MEANING	English Words
sect	cut	section جزء
simil	like	similar مشابه
tele	far away	television
tempor	time	temporary مؤقت
theo	god	theology علم اللاهوت
therm	heat	thermal حراري
uni	one	union اتحاد
vac	empty	vacant شاغر
verb	word	verbal لفظى
vol	wish,willing	volunteer متطوع
volv	roll	evolve يطور
soph	wisdom	sophistry سفسطة
ann	year	annual سنوى

Compound Words (الكلمات المركبة)

(10) الكلمات المركبة هى عبارة عن كلمتين متصلتين ، ومن الصعوبة معرفة استخدام الفاصلة من عدم استخدامها ، وهناك اختلاف دائم بين الإنجليزية البريطانية ونظيرتها الأمريكية ، وهناك تباين أيضا بين القواميس المختلفة داخل أى من الدولتين تجاه استخدام الفاصلة ، واستخدام الفاصلة فى الإنجليزية الأمريكية أقل بكثير من الإنجليزية البريطانية .

الأمثلة :

تكتب ككلمة واحدة	تكتب مع فاصلة	تكتب ككلمتين منفصلتين
firsthand	first-degree	First aid
landholder	land-poor	land office
postgraduate	post-morton	post meridian

اشتقاقات الكلمة :

(1) من اسم إلى صفة :

Noun	Adjective
beauty	beautiful
self	selfish
harmony	harmonious متناغم harmonic متآلف

(2) من صفة إلى اسم :

Adjective	Noun
selfish	selfishness
harmonious, harmonic	harmoniousness

(3) من صفة أو اسم إلى ظرف :

Adjective	Noun	Adverb
beautiful	beauty	beautifully
selfish	selfishness	selfishly

(4) من اسم أو صفة إلى فعل :

Adjective	Noun	Adverb
beauty	beautiful	beautify
harmoniousness	harmonious	harmonize

Verb	Noun
beautify	beautification, beautifier
harmonize	harmonization, harmonizer

النفي (negation)

(1) من خلال prefix :

un -	unselfish	(adj)
	unselfishly	(adv)
dis -	disharmony (n)	
in -	inharmonious (adj)	
in	harmoniousness (noun)	

ملحوظة : نضع فاصلة بعد كلمة self عندما تأتي كسابقة ببداية الكلمة فيما عدا كلمة selfhood.

***

(1) تجنب التكرار لنفس الفكرة بكلمات مختلفة ، وتجنب التعبيرات الشائعة مع المحددات التى لا تضيف معنى ، والكلمات التالية غير ضرورية بعد السابقة عليها.

return (back)	combine (together)
repeat (again)	(personal) friend
(past) histroy	(mistaken) error
each (and every) one	(final) outcome
many (in number)	(necessary) essentials
large (in size)	(optional) choice
early (in time)	(end) result

(2) تجنب شبه الجمل غير الضرورية وخاصة العبارات التى تبدأ بـ of

Reduce	Wordy	to	improved
	the house of the Johnsons		the Johnsons' house
	one of the purposes		one purpose
	one of the results		one result
	two ot the reasons		two reasons
	several of the students		several students
	height of five feet		five feet high
	weight of ten pounds		ten pounds
	he potatoes are ten pounds in weight		the potatoes weigh ten pounds

Wordy	improved
with the exception of	except
in this day and age	today, now
at the present time	today, now
at this point in time	today, now
at that point in time	then
in regard to	about
by the time (that)	when
subsequent to	after
before long	soon
during the time (that)	while

(3) استخدم الصيغة القصيرة ، حينما يمكن التعبير عن الفكرة بكلمة واحدة أو بعبارة.

Wordy	improved
as a result of	because of
in the event (that)	if
on condition (that)	if
provided, providing (that)	if
due to the fact (that)	since
inasmuch as	since
in view of the fact (that)	since
prior to	before

(4) تجنب استخدام الكلمات التي ليس لها معنى ولا تضيف شيئاً جديداً ،

وهى تأتى فى صدر الجملة وتسمى expletives

Wordy : There are four books that Bill needs from the library.

Improved : Bill needs four books from the library.

Wordy : There are several buses that are waiting in the parking lot.

Improved : Several buses are waiting in the parking lot.

(5) قلل من عدد الكلمات من خلال تغيير التركيب النحوى فى الجملة ، وقلل جملتين أو أكثر إلى جملة واحدة .

Wordy : Will is a basketball player. He is the captain of his team. He is the best player, too.

Improved : Will, the captain, plays basketball better than anyone else in his team.

Improved : Will , the captain of his basketball team, is its best player.

Wordy : Diane plays tennis every day. She hopes that she will be able to play in the tournament for the whole state. It will take place next summer.

Improved : Playing tennis every day, Diane is training for the state tournament next summer.

ENGLISH
WITHOUT
MISTAKES

Prepositions

حروف الجر

إن حروف الجر من الصعوبات التى تواجه معظم الدارسين للغة الإنجليزية، وتكمن الصعوبة فى أن الطالب يتعلم اسماً أو صفة أو فعلاً جديداً مع معرفة حرف الجر المتصل بالكلمة إذا كان الأمر يحتاج إلى ذلك وفى معظم الأحيان يؤدى التخمين أو التعميم فى اختيار حرف الجر المناسب إلى الوقوع فى الخطأ، وهذا بدوره يعود إلى أن الطالب يحاول أن يجد حرف الجر المناسب من خلال لغته الأم ، وعلى سبيل المثال ، اختر حرف الجر المناسب للفعل admit to ومعناه يعترف بـ / يقر بـ ستجد أن مقابل حرف الجر «بـ» فى الإنجليزية هو with وليس to .

سأحاول من خلال هذا الفصل أن أقدم عرضاً لحروف الجر المختلفة، وكيفية استخدامها ، كما أستطيع القول إنه من خلال هذا الفصل يتسنى لك كيفية الاستخدام الصحيح لحروف الجر المتنوعة ، وقبل الولوج فى عمق الموضوع، أود فى البداية أن أعرض عليك أيها القارئ العزيز حروف الجر الشائعة فى اللغة الإنجليزية ، وفى حقيقة الأمر حرف الجر ليس له معنى ثابت تستطيع أن تجزم به حيث أن معناه يتغير حسب علاقته بالفعل أو الصفة أو الاسم السابق عليه .

82   English without

٨٢

حروف الجر : Prepositions

from	by
in	concerning
inside	despite
into	down
like	during
near	past
of	regard
on	since
out of	through
over	along
throughout	among
till	around
to	at
towards	before
under	behind
underneath	below
until	beneath
unto up	beside
upon	besides
with	between
within	beyond
without	but
about	except
above	for
during	
past	
regard	

away from بعيدًا عن	conformably to وفقًا لـ
according to وفقًا لـ	in place of عوضًا عن
alongside of جنبًا إلى جنب مع	in according حسب
agreeably to منسجمًا مع	in addition بالإضافة
along with جنبًا إلى جنب مع	in lieu of بدلًا من
instead of بدلًا من	in compliance امتثالًا
in comparison to مقارنة بـ	by virtue of استنادًا إلى
in case of في حالة	by way of عن طريق
in course of في سياق	
in order to لأجل	
in regard to فيما يتعلق	
in favour في صالح	
owing to بسبب	
by dint of بفضل	
by means of بواسطة	
on account of لأجل	
with reference بالإشارة	
up to لحد	
with a view بغية	
with a view to على أمل أن	
with an eye to تطلعًا إلى	
with regard to بالنسبة إلى	

aim يهدف إلى	good جيد في	scoff يسخر من
alarmed قلق من	laugh يضحك على	skilful ماهر في
angry (at something) غضبان من	look ينظر إلى	stare at يحملق في
annoyed متضايق من	mock يسخر من	surprised مندهش من
arrive يصل إلى	peep يختلس النظر	throw يرمي في
bad سيئ في	pleased (at a thing) سعيد من	preside (to be ahead of) يترأس
clever ماهر في	preside (to be ahead of) يترأس	wink يغمز لـ
call (to visit a place) يزور	rejoice يبتهج من	work يعمل في
disgusted مشمئز من	sad حزين من	

avenge ينتقم من	depend يعتمد على	put يضع على
act أثر في	feed يتغذى على	rely يعتمد على
call (on a person) يدعو	focus يركز على	revenge ينتقم من
concentrate يركز على	insist يصر على	spend ينفق على
	live يعيش على - على الهواء	wait (to serve) يخدم

متهم بـ accuse	composed يتألف من	hatred كراهية في
afraid خائف من	conscious مدرك لـ (ك\ارك)	hear يسمع بـ
approve يوافق على	consist يتكون من	hopeful أمل في
ashamed خجول من	cure يشفى من	ignorant جاهل بـ
aware مطلع على	deprive يحرم من	ill مريض بـ
beware جدار من	despair ييأس من	inform يخبر بـ
boast يتباهى بـ	die يموت من	innocent برئ من
capable قادر على	fond مغرم بـ	instead بدلاً من
careful دقيق في	free خال من	jealous غيور من
certain متأكد من	full ملئ بـ	love يحب
come (result from) ينتج عن	glad (grateful) سعيد بـ	(in) need بحاجة إلى
complain يشكو من	guilty مذنب في	proud فخور بـ
repent يقدم على	sure متأكد من	tired متعب من
(in) search يبحث عن	suspect يشك في	warn يحذر من
independent مستقل عن	think يفكر في	weary سئم/ مل من

act (represent) العمل من أجل	fit ملائم لـ	respect احترام لـ
anxious حريص على	good (suitable) جيد في	responsible مسئول عن
ask يطلب	hatred كراهية لـ	sail يبحر إلى
bad (hurtful) سيئ	jealous غيور على	send (order) يرسل إلى
beg يلتمس من	leave for يرحل إلى	sorry أسف لـ
care يهتم بـ	long يتوق إلى	stand يشح لـ
cry يبكي	love يحب	suitable ملائم لـ

يقوم do	يخطئ mistake	يصوت لـ vote
يصرف exchange	يحتاج need	ينتظر لـ wait
شهير بـ famous	مستعد لـ ready	

كلمات يتبعها حرف الجر with

يزخر بـ abound	يتآمر مع conspire	يتنازل عن part
ملم بـ acquainted	يتشاور مع consult	pleased (with a person)
		مسرور بـ
يتفق مع agree	يتغلب على cope	يزود بـ provide
يغضب angry (with person)	يغطي بـ cover	يتشاجر مع quarrel
من		
يجادل argue	اتفاق مع deal	راض عن satisfied
حريص careful	يناقش مع discuss	sympathize
		يتعاطف مع
يقارن compare	يستغني عن dispense	يتلاعب بـ tamper
يمتثل لـ comply	يمتلئ بـ fill	

كلمات يتبعها حرف الجر in

abound	sell	يفشل في fail
يستغرق في absorbed	confidence	يملأ fill
يصل إلى arrive	deal (buy and sell)	مهتم بـ interested
يؤمن بـ believe	disappointed	ينجح في succeed
		مستاء من
يشتري buy	يرتدي dress	

يختلف عن differ	يحمي من protect	يعاني من suffer
يتعادل في draw	يتسلم من receive	ينتج عن result
خال من free	recover	
	يتعافى من	

كلمات يتبعها حرف الجر about

قلق من anxious	متشكك في doubtful	يتكلم عن speak
يسأل عن ask	يتغاضى عن forget	قلق على worried
يحرص على care	يقرأ عن read	
يشك في doubt		

كلمات يتبعها حرف الجر into

يدخل في break into	يستوعب get	يترجم translate
ينفجر في burst	يبدأ go	يتحول turn
يتحول إلى change	يخاطب run	

لاحظ واقرأ بعناية حروف الجر التى تشير إلى المكان:

in

........in Canada (any country), in Alexandria (any city), in Clordo Castle of province
), in Room 261 or an apartment 210 A (specific room or an apartment), in a
dormitory, in a apartment, in house , in student hostel, in poverty, in wealth, in
a city , in a suburb, in a town, in a village, in the south, in the west, (region or
section) in a collage , in the mountains, in the desert, in a forest, int a field, in a
garden, in bed , in a hospital, in a prison

, in a square, in the picture.

لاحظ أننا نقول :

in ....

the water, a river , a row , a line , a queue, the sky, the street

يقول الأمريكيون : on the street

at ....

at 261 Green Arenue (street with a number), at Doha airport, at the university, at the shore, at The Chicago airport, at home , at school, at Work, at the office, at the bus stop, at the door, at the window, at the top/ bottom, at the back, at the supermarket, at crossroads, at the reception.

on ....

on Green Arenue (street without a number), on a farm, on the beach, on the ocean , on the river, on the bay , on the lake, on the plains, on the floor, on the ground, on the grass, on the table, on the left, on the right, on the way.

لاحظ واقرأ بعناية حروف الجر التى تشير إلى الزمن :

in ....

in time for class, in 1980 (year), in May (month), in the morning, in the evening, daytime, the night, in the past ten years, in the past decade, in few minutes, in a week.

at ....

at ten O'clock (specific time), at noon, at midnight, at night, at lunch time, at dawn, at the week end, at Christmas, at the moment, at present , at the same time, at the age of, at dusk, at sunset.

ON ·············
▼

On time, on the hour, on the minute, on the day , on may 18 (date) on Wednesday
(day of the week), on Christmas day, on Friday morning/ evening (s) afternoon
(s) / evening (s) night (s) .

ملاحظات حول بعض حروف الجر:

(1) استخدام حرف الجر of يشير إلى جزء من الكل (لاحظ أنه عندما تأتي one قبل of ، فـ one هو فاعل
الجملة ويأخذ فعلاً في صيغة المفرد ، حتى لو كان الاسم بعد of جمعاً) .

الأمثلة :

(1) One of our friends has a car.

(2) One of the best methods is the one that you used yesterday.

* ولكن عند الإشارة إلى اسم لا يجمع ، تكون الجملة كالآتي :

مثال :

: Much of the water is polluted.

** يجب أن تستبدل أسماء الجمع بضمائر جمع كالآتي :

الأمثلة:

: One of them has a car .

: Many of them have cars.

: Ten of them are missing.

: Some of them are here.

* قد يتبع of اسم لا يعد ومن الممكن استبداله بالضمير كالآتي:

: Some of the rice (it) has been burned.

 : Much of the advice (it) that I get is useless.

 : All of the news (it) is good today.

 : None of the information (it) was helpful.

 : Chris is a doctor of Dentistry

 : Atef is a professor of Biology.

(2) لاحظ هذه الاستخدامات لـ of / out of / from للإشارة إلى النسب أو مادة الشيء.. الأمثلة :

 : Rashid is a citizen of Qater.

 : Mohamed is a student from Egypt. * (His home is in Egypt).

 : George is a student of Egypt. (His studies about Egypt).

 : They are resident of the United States.

 : Khalid is a doctor from Giza .

 : The desk is made of/from/out of wood.

 : This jam is made of /from/ out of strawberry.

 : This cloth comes from India. It is made of/from/ out of silk.

 : Butter is made of / from/ out of cream.

* من الممكن أن تشير of أيضاً إلى المادة أو المحتوى كالآتى :

الأمثلة :

: We bought a basket of tomatoes . (Tomatoes were in the basket).

 : We bought a basket of straw. (The basket is made of straw).

(3) استخدم for لبيان الغرض كالآتى:

الأمثلة :

 : Mostafa is going for an interview tomorrow.

 : Emad needs a new case for his camera.

(4) استخدم on و about لبيان الفاعل كالآتى :

الأمثلة :

 : I just bought a book on/about/archaeology.

 : Felix has read many of articles on/about architecture.

(5) استخدم except و but لبيان الحذف كالآتى :

الأمثلة:

 : No one but/except Ahmed saw the new schedule.

 : Everyone is ready except/ but Gassim.

(6) استخدم by و with لبيان الفاعل واستخدم without لبيان عدم وجود الفاعل .

الأمثلة:

: They travelled by car/plane/train/etc.

: The small boy tied his shoes by himself. (With no help from anyone).

(7) استخدم because of / on account of و due to / owing to لبيان السبب أو الداعى .

(8) الأمثلة :

Owing to
Due to
On account of ⊢·····his age/he could get the job he wanted.
Because of

* لاحظ الفرق بين because of و because ، حيث أن (because) يتبعها دائماً جملة تتكون من فاعل وفعل ، أما (because of)، فهى حرف جر مركب ويتبعها اسم.

الأمثلة:

 : Because of he was too young, he could not get the job he wanted.

 :Because of his under-age, he could not get the job he wanted.

(8) استخدم besides و as well as و together with لإضافة أفكار أو معلومات.

الأمثلة:

 : Three teams besides / in addition / together with / as well as ours played in the tournament.

besides هى أفضل اختيار لتجنب الإفراط فى استعمال الكلمات.

(9) استخدم in spite of و despite لبيان الإقرار بشيء كالآتى:

الأمثلة:

 : In Spite of the bad weather, our trip to the mountain was a success.

 : Despite Many people are cheerful in spite of their problems.

(10) استخدم like لبيان التشابه ، أما as فتستخدم فقط كحرف جر عندما تعنى in

the role of وما عدا ذلك فهى أداة ربط .

الأمثلة:

: Like father, like son.

: He looks like his father, walks like his father and eats like his father.

: Now I am speaking not as (حرف جر) your doctor but as (حرف جر) your friend.

: She is not as (أداة ربط) friendly as her brother

(11) لا تخلط بين to كحرف جر مع to التى تسبق مصدر الفعل.

الأمثلة:

: Sometimes it is difficult to get the dirver's license.

: It is not easy to learn another language.

: He failed due to the lack of experience.

(12) كثيراً ما تستخدم حروف الجر التى تشير إلى المكان بأسلوب بلاغى لبيان الروابط المنطقية كالآتى :

الأمثلة:

: What are the reason behind our proposal?

: They value their freedom above all else.

: The costs have gone beyond the estimate.

Participial Preposition (13)

هناك بعض صيغ الكلمات والتى يضاف لنهايتها ing قد يأتى بعضها أسماء أو ضمائر فى تركيب لغوى متشابه مع شبه الجملة .

الأمثلة:

: Barring (a part from) a delay, the package should arrive

Monday.

 : Concerning your parking violation , you will have to pay the fine by the date below

 : Considering (taking into account) the quality, the price is not high.

 : Not with standing (= in the spite of) of resistance, he was arrested.

 : Regarding your inquiries, we regret saying that we do not have photocopier accessories.

 : Touching (=with regard to) this matter , I have not taken a decision.

تستخدم العديد من الكلمات أحياناً كظروف وأحياناً أخرى كحروف جر ، ولمعرفة الاختلاف ، فالظرف يشير دائماً إلى حركة الفعل ، أما حرف الجر فهو لتحديد الاسم أو الضمير الذى يشير إليه .

الأمثلة:

Preposition	Adverb
(1) Ali is waiting outside the door.	Ali is waiting ouside
(2) The taxi was waiting near the hotel	The taxi was waiting nearby
(3) I couldn't come before.	I came the day before yesterday.
(4) The book is on the table.	Let us move on.
(5) His father arrived soon after.	After a month, he arrived.

Varied Idiomatic Expressions and their Different Meanings.

(1) pave the way for. يمهد الطريق لـ

We pave the way for the next generations.

نمهد الطريق للأجيال القادمة.

(2) fell in love. وقع في الحب

He fell in love with her at first sight.

وقع في حبها من أول نظرة.

(3) lose sight of. يغيب عن البال

We must not lose sight of our aim.

لا ينبغى أن يغيب الهدف من حياتنا .

(4) in the short/ long run. على المدى البعيد

This will be important in the short / long run.

سيكون لذلك أهمية على المدى القصير / البعيد

(5) get off my back. ينصرف عن

I wish they would get off my back.

أتمنى التخلص من مضايقتهم .

(6) at stake. في خطر

His decision put our company at stake.

وضع قراره الشركة في خطر .

(7) at the peak of في ذروة

Mary is at the peak of her career.

مارى فى ذروة مستواها الوظيفى .

(8) on the verge of tears على وشك البكاء

The child was on the verge of tears.

أوشك الطفل على البكاء

(9) at the age of في عمر

He died at the age of sixty.

مات في عمر الستين

(10) from hand to mouth على الكفاف

He lives from hand to mouth.

يعيش على الكفاف

(11) on good/ bad terms with على علاقة طيبة/ سيئة مع

John is on good/ bad terms with his neighbours.

جون على علاقة حسنة / سيئة مع جيرانه.

(12) for free مجاناً

I got this ticket for free.

حصلت على هذه التذكرة مجاناً.

(13) to the letter بحذافيرها

Tom carries out orders to the letter.

نفذ توم الأوامر بحذافيرها (بالحرف الواحد).

(14) on the right/wrong track في المسار الصحيح/الخطأ

I am sure we are on the right / wrong track.

أنا متأكد أننا في المسار الصحيح / الخطأ.

(15) in question الذي نحن بصدده

The problem in question is very complicated.

المشكلة التي نحن بصددها معقدة جداً.

(16) to the core في الصميم

Shawki is Egyptian to the core.

شوقى مصرى صميم (فى صميمه).

(17) at one stroke في الحال

Fifty men were killed at one stroke at once).

قتل خمسون شخصاً فى الحال (فى لمح البصر).

(18) at well حسب الرغبة

You can not have everything changed at well.

لا يمكنك تغيير كل شيء كيفما (حسبما) تريد .

(19) on one measure حسب معيار واحد

You can compare the two groups on one measure.

يمكن مقارنة المجموعتين حسب معيار واحد .

(20) in return for مقابل

He did this in return for money.

قام بعمل ذلك مقابل المال .

(21) waging a war يشن حرباً

The police are waging a war against / on crime in the city.

يشن البوليس حرباً ضد الجريمة فى المدينة .

(22) by mistake بالخطأ

He took my bag by mistake.

أخذ حقيبتى عن طريق الخطأ.

(23) by force بالقوة

The thief took the money from the lady by force.

أخذ المال من السيدة بالقوة .

(24) beyond compare لا مثيل له/ لها

She is beyond compare.

ليس لها مثيل.

(25) take revenge on ينتقم من

He wants to have/get/take revenge on his enemy.

يريد الانتقام من عدوه .

(26) take pride in يعتز بـ

He takes pride in his success.

يزهو (يعتز) بنجاحه .

(27) take into account يأخذ في الحسبان/ يضع في الاعتبار

Don't forget to take this into account.

لا تنس أن تضع هذا في اعتبارك .

(28) take into consideration يأخذ بعين الاعتبار

I always take other's opinions into consideration when facing a defficult problem.

دائماً أضع في اعتباري آراء الآخرين عند مواجهة مشكلة عويصة .

(29) at the expense of على حساب

We had a meal at the expense of the headmaster.

تناولنا وجبة على نفقة الناظر (مدير المدرسة) .

(30) in agood health بصحة جيدة

Karim is in a good health.

كريم بصحة جيدة .

(31) by surprise على حين غرة

Rebels took the town by surprise.

فاجأ المتمردون المدينة / أخذ المتمردون المدينة على حين غِرَّة.

(32) at issue موضوع النقاش

What's at issue here is the future of industry.

موضوع المناقشة هو مستقبل الصناعة.

(33) at last/ lenght أخيراً

At last / length, the bus arrived twenty minutes late.

وأخيراً، وصل الأتوبيس بعد عشرين دقيقة من ميعاده.

(34) at the mercy of تحت رحمة

The ship at the mercy of the storm.

كانت السفينة رهن / تحت رحمة العاصفة.

(35) feel like يشعر بـ

Mary felt like a fish out of water at the party.

شعرت ماري بالغربة وهي في الحفل.

(36) at hearth في الصميم

He is a countryman at heart.

ابن بلد من صميمه / (من صميم قلبه/ أعماقه).

(37) by heart عن ظهر قلب

Alaa learnt the whole list by heart.

حفظ علاء القائمة عن ظهر قلب.

(38) at the top of بأعلى

She shouted at the top of her voice.

صرخت بأعلى صوتها.

(39) daggers at بعين

She looked daggers at me.

نظرت إليّ بعين الغضب.

(40) in hand في حوزة

I still have some money in hand.

ما زال في حوزتي بعض المال.

(41) bit by bit شيئًا فشيئًا/تدريجيًا

He saved the money bit by bit until he had enough to buy a car.

وفر المال تدريجياً حتى يكون لديه ما يكفيه لشراء سيارة.

(42) in charge of مسئول عن

Tom is in charge of the factory.

يتولى توم مسئولية المصنع.

(43) in the course of بمرور

Everything will get better in the course of time.

سوف يتحسن كل شيء مع مرور الوقت.

(44) in regard to فيما يتعلق

After October War 1973 there was a dramatic shift in Israel in regard to international legitimacy and the right of self-determination for Palestinian People .

بعد حرب أكتوبر عام 1973 ، حدث تحول درامى في إسرائيل فيما يتعلق بالشرعية الدولية وحق تقرير المصير للشعب الفلسطينى.

(45) in an effect to في محاولة

He will analyze the date in an effect to learn what happened.

سوف يجرى تحليلاً للبيانات في محاولة لمعرفة ما حدث.

(46) for granted يسلم جدلًا

Don't take anything for granted.

لا تسلم بصحة أى شيء.

(47) came into effect سيدخل حيز التنفيذ

The new rule will come / be brought / be put / go into effect on Sunday.

ستدخل اللائحة الجديدة حيز التنفيذ يوم الأحد.

(48) in effect ساري المفعول

The rules will remain in effect till October

سيبقى العمل باللوائح ساري المفعول حتى أكتوبر.

(49) at peace with في وئام مع

You should be at peace with yourself.

يجب أن تكون في وئام مع النفس / تصالح مع الذات.

(50) take over يستولي على

They will not take my money over my dead body.

لن يأخذوا نقودي إلا على جثتي.

(51) one foot in على وشك

The old man has one foot in the grave.

أوشك الشيخ العجوز على الموت.

(52) on equal terms with على نفس العلاقة

She is on equal terms with her ex-boss.

هي على نفس درجة العلاقة مع مديرها السابق.

(53) in hand لدى

Do you have any pen in hand?

هل لديك / معك أى قلم؟

(54) on the safe side في مأمن

I will take more money to be on the safe side.

سآخذ معى مالاً أكثر كى أكون في مأمن من العواقب.

(55) take part in يشارك

Both Ihab and Mohamed will take part in school activity.

سيشارك كل من إيهاب ومحمد فى أنشطة المدرسة.

(56) take advantage of يستغل

We have to take advantage of this long holiday.

ينبغى أن نغتنم هذه الإجازة الطويلة.

(57) behind the time رجعي

Tom's dogmatic thinking makes him behind the time.

تفكير توم المتشدد يجعله رجعيًّا.

(58) in your shoes مكانك/محلك

If I were in your shoes, I would marry Dalia.

لو كنت فى مكانك لتزوجت داليا.

(59) on credit على الحساب بالمديونية

I will buy this car on credit.

سأشترى هذه السيارة على الحساب.

(60) on edge about متوتر

Ahmed seems to be on edge about something.

يبدو أن أحمد متوتر لشيء ما.

(61) in advance مسبقًا

You have to make hotel reservation in advance.

يجب عمل الحجز مقدماً.

(62) up to my ears منهمك

I am up to my ears in work.

إنني منهمك فى العمل.

(63) get rid of يتخلص من

She has to get rid of her mistakes.

لابد أن تتخلص من أخطائها.

(64) put in a word يزكي

I hope Jassim will put in a word for me.

آمل في تزكية / توصية من جاسم.

(65) put in يلتمس

The lawyer´s defence put her in the clear.

برأها دفاع المحامي من التهمة.

(66) under the weather متوعك

I feel under the weather , so I think I'll go to bed early.

أشعر بوعكة، ومن ثم أرى أن أخلد للنوم مبكرًا.

(67) from bad to worse من سيئ لأسوأ

Our company is going from bad to worse.

سار وضع الشركة من سيئ إلى أسوأ.

(68) to the point صميم

Why don't you come to the point.

لماذا تدخل في صميم الموضوع.

(69) from now on من الآن فصاعدًا

From Now on I must treat him kindly.

من الآن فصاعداً ، لابد أن أعامله برفق.

(70) leave for يرحل

Nader will leave Qatar for good.

سيرحل نادر من قطر للأبد.

(71) in her toes في يقظة

She was in her toes in the interview.

كانت في يقظة في المقابلة.

(72) come down يعاني = suffer

Naser is coming down with the flu.

يعاني ناصر من الإنفلونزا.

(73) willing to لدي رغبة في/ مستعد

I never used a computer before, but I am willing to try.

لم يسبق لى استخدام الكمبيوتر مطلقاً لكن لدي رغبة في المحاولة.

(74) a far cry from بعيدة كل البعد-هوة كبيرة

Hani's ideas are a far cry from mine.

هناك ثمة تفاوت كبير بين أفكار هانى وأفكارى .

ملاحظات:

(1) ربما يتبع الكلمة حرفان من حروف الجر دون أى تغيير فى المعنى . الأمثلة :

(a) The noise comes from across the river.

(b) I sold my car for under it's half cost.

(c) Each article was sold at over a pound.

(2) ربما يتبع نفس الكلمة حرفان من حروف الجر مع حدوث تغيير فى المعنى لكل حالة ، وبناء عليك الرجوع إلى القاموس لمعرفة درجة الاختلاف .

: (A) Shrief is jealous of Marwa.

أ- يغار شريف من مروة (بمعنى أنه يكرهها) .

: (B) Shrief is jealous for Marwa.

ب- يغار شريف على مروة (بمعنى أنه واقع فى غرامها) .

: Hassan is anxious about his son.

ج- حسن قلق على ابنه .

: Hassan is anxious for his son.

يشتاق حسن إلى رؤية ابنه .

(3) هناك بعض الأفعال التى يتبعها حرف جر فى اللغة العربية ، ولكن لا يأتى بعدها أى حرف فى اللغة الإنجليزية وإليك أمثلة من هذه الأفعال .

(أ) admire يعجب بـ

 Hassan admires Niveen

يعجب حسن بنيفين

(ب) affect يؤثر على

The news affected him.

أثرت الأنباء فى نفسه .

(ج) approash يقترب من / يدنو من

We approached the ministry buliding.

اقتربنا من مبنى الوزارة .

(4) arrest يقبض على

: The policeman arrested the criminal

قبضت الشرطة على المجرم .

(5) attack يهجم على

: our army attacked the enemy

هجم جيشنا على العدو .

(6) contain يحتوى على

: The building contains many rooms.

تحتوى / تشتمل العمارة على كثير من الحجرات .

(7) celebrate يحتفل بـ

: We celebrate the new year with out friends.

احتفلنا بمقدم العام الجديد مع أصدقائنا .

(8) defend يدافع عن

: We must defend our rights and interests.

يجب أن ندافع عن حقوقنا ومصالحنا .

(9) enjoy يستمتع بـ

: I enjoyed Adel Emam's film.

استمتعت بفيلم لعادل إمام .

(10) fear يخاف من

: The boy feared the dog.

خاف الصغير من الكلب.

(11) feel يشعر بـ

: I feel sad.

أشعر بأننى حزين.

(12) fulfil يفي بـ

: Shehab fulfilled his promise and came early.

وفى شهاب بوعده وجاء مبكراً.

(13) get يحصل على

: He got full marks in English.

حصل على الدرجة النهائية فى اللغة الإنجليزية.

(14) join يلحق بـ

: Tamer joined the faculty of medicine last year.

التحق تامر بكلية الطب العام الماضى .

(15) keep يحافظ على

: You must keep your promises

يجب أن تحافظى على وعودك (تفى بوعودك).

(16) need يحتاج إلى

: Shrouk needs a lot of money to buy a car

تحتاج شروق إلى كثير من المال لشراء سيارة .

(17) obtain يحصل على

: I have not been able to obtain the book anywhere.

لم أستطع الحصول على الكتاب من أى مكان.

: They recognized his musical ability.

عرفوا إمكاناته الموسيقية

(19) risk يخاطر بـ

 : Don't risk your future.

لا تخاطر بمستقبلك .

(20) sacrifice يضحى بـ

 : My mother sacrificed herself for us.

ضحت أمى بنفسها من أجلنا .

Vocabulary
مفردات

سأتناول بإذن الله تعالى فى هذا الفصل، المعانى الصحيحة لبعض المفردات، والتى يقع فى خطأ استخدامها الاستخدام الصحيح عديد من الطلبة والدارسين، بسبب الاختلافات البسيطة فى المعنى وفى شكل اللغة بما يخدع كل الدارسين، ويزيد من حيرتهم فى استخدام المعنى السليم ، وسأعرض لكيفية استخدام هذه المفردات على طريقة العبارة الشهيرة فى لغتنا العربية الجميلة «قل ولا تقل» وهى كالآتى :

Don't Say : We went to the cinema altogether.

Say : We went to the cinema all together.

ملاحظة :

لاحظ أن (altogether) تعنى :(تماماً) / أما (all together) فتعنى «معاً» وهى عكس separately

Don't Say : Tom gave his exam.

Say : Tom took his exam.

Note : (A) The student (takes) or (sits) for the exam.

(B) The teacher (gives) or sits the exam.

Don't Say : Tom did many mistakes in the exam.

Say : Tom made many mistakes in the exam.

ملاحظة: لاحظ الاستخدامات المختلفة للفعل do و الفعل make

أمثلة :

Examples : We do our homework, housework, cooking, dishes, exercise, (our) best.

We make effort, a meal, (our) beds, mistakes.

Don't Say : The boy fell in love head on heels.

Say : The boy fell in love head over heels.

☆ Don't Say : Don't play duck and drake with your money.

☆ Say : Don't play ducks and drakes with your money.

☆ Don't Say : You passed in life with fire and water.

☆ Say : You passed in life through fire and water.

☆ Don't Say : People collect money with hook or with crook.

☆ Say : People collect money by hook or by crook.

☆ Dont't Say : I don't know how to keep the wolf from my doors.

☆ Say: I don't know how to keep the wolf away from my doors.

☆ Dont't Say : Jane tries to arrive to / secure her ambition.

☆ Say : Jane tries to attain / realize / fulfil / achieve her ambition.

☆ Don't Say : Bassil will realize a compromise with the company .

☆ Say : Bassil will reach / achieve a compromise with the company .

☆ Don't Say : The river is profound.

☆ Say : The river is deep.

☆ Dont't Say : Mostafa made me a small discount.

☆ Say : Mostafa allowed / gave me a small discount.

☆ Don't Say : Don't put fuel on the fire.

☆ Say : Don't put fuel to the fire.

✩ Don't Say : What is being cooked here .

✩ Say : What is cooked up here.

✩ Don't Say : Please read the letter between each line.

✩ Say : Please read the letter between the line.

✩ Don't Say :You are of colour today.

✩ Say :You are off colour today.

✩ Don't Say :You must stand upon point.

✩ Say :You must stand upon points.

✩ Don't Say :My child saw a bad dream last night.

✩ Say : My child had a bad dream last night.

✩ Don't Say : We kept quite.

✩ Say : We kept quiet.

✩ Don't Say : Tamim ran very fastly .

✩ Say :Tamim ran very fast.

✩ Don't Say : I am shy of my mistakes.

✩ Say : I am ashamed of my mistakes.

✩ Don't Say : Let us bury the hatchets .

✩ Say : Let us bury the hatchet.

✩ Don't Say :Don't build a castle on air.

✩ Say :Don't build a castle in the air.

✩ Don't Say : She moved heavens and earths to get the job.

✩ Say :She moved heaven and earth to get the job.

✩ Don't Say : Life is not a plot of roses.

✩ Say : Life is not a bed of roses.

✩ Don't Say : A practical man swims with the tides.

✩ Say : A practical man swims with the tide.

☼ Don't Say : You are between the fire.

☼ Say : You are between two fires.

☼ Don't Say : The enemy took to their heals.

☼ Say : The enemy took to their heal.

☼ Don't Say : It makes my mouth watered.

☼ Say : It makes my mouth water.

☼ Don't Say : I wish to know how it happened precisely .

☼ Say : I wish to know how precisely it happened.

☼ Don't Say : The above account is wrong.

☼ Say : The account above is worng.

☼ Don't Say : I had met late prime minister Kamal Al - Ganzori .

☼ Say : I had met the ex-prime minister Kamal Al - Ganzori.

☼ Don't Say : He was little tired.

☼ Say : He was a little tired.

☼ Don't Say : I met him particular.

☼ Say : I met him in particular.

☼ Don't Say : Cholera has broken her.

☼ Say : Cholera has broken out her.

☼ Don't Say: He set on his journey.

☼ Say : He set out on his journey.

☼ Don't Say: The patient will be good soon.

☼ Say: The patient will be well soon.

☼ Don't Say: He dead.

☼ Say : He died or he is / was dead.

☼ Don't Say : She feels alone after her husband's death.

☼ Say : She feels lonely after her husband's death .

☞ Don't Say : Ali borrows me his pen .

☞ Say : Ali lent me his pen .

☞ Don't Say : He remembers me with my father.

☞ Say : He reminds me with my father .

☞ Don't Say : The murder was hung last week .

☞ Say : The murder was hanged last week .

☞ Don't Say : A gang stole the bank last week .

☞ Say : A gang robbed the bank last week .

☞ Don't Say : Ayman robbed our money .

☞ Say : Ayman stole our money .

☞ Don't Say : This is cause why I don't like him .

☞ Say : This is why I don't like him .

☞ Don't Say : It was a clouded day .

☞ Say : It was a cloudy day .

☞ Don't Say : She let the house from Mrs. Amira .

☞ Say : She rented the house from Mrs. Amira.

☞ Don't Say : We agreed to his proposal .

☞ Say : We accepted his proposal .

☞ Don't Say : Mohamed has to by very economic .

☞ Say : Mohamed has to be very economical .

☞ Don't Say : The actor's performance enjoyed me .

☞ Say : The actor's performance amused / pleased me .

☞ Don't Say : The boat was drowned in the river .

☞ Say : The boat was sunk in the river .

☞ Don't Say : Malik is learning at Cairo University .

☞ Say : Malik is studing at Cairo University.

Articles
الأدوات النحوية

تنقسم الأدوات النحوية إلى قسمين (أ) أداتا النكرة a/an . (ب) أداة معرفة the تستخدم أداتا النكرة /a
an قبل الأسماء المفردة التى تعد فقط ، أما أداة المعرفة the فقد تستخدم أمام الأسماء التى لا تعد وأسماء
الجمع التى تعد أيضاً ، والأدوات النحوية تحدد عمل الاسم الذى يتلوها وتأتى سابقة على الاسم التالى لها .

أداتا النكرة   The Indefinite Articles

القاعدة (1) استخدم أداة النكرة «a» إذا كان الاسم التالى لها اسماً يعد ويبدأ بحرف ساكن . الأمثلة :

a car, a pen , a book , a radio.

استثناءات : إذا بدأت الكلمة بـ eu أو u وتنطق على أنها u مثل ، university , European , unit فضع
قبلها أداة النكرة «a» .

القاعدة (2) استخدم «a» قبل Mr /.Miss/Mrs + اسم الشخص إذا كان الشخص غريباً وغير مألوف .
الأمثلة :

A Mr, Mohammed, a Miss Dalia, A Mrs. Mushira.

شخص يدعى (محمد)- سيدة تدعى (داليا)- سيدة تدعى (مشيرة).

القاعدة (3) استخدم أداة النكرة «an» قبل الاسم الذى يعد ويبدأ بحرف متحرك . الأمثلة :

An eagle. an office, an orange, an apple.

استثناءات : إذا بدأ الاسم بحرف «h» غير منطوق فاستخدم أداة النكرة «an» . الأمثلة :

an hour, an honest man

القاعدة (4) نستخدم some مع الأسماء التى لا تعد وليس a أو an . الأمثلة :

١١٤

(1) He wants some rice.

 (2) He is taking some instruction in music now.

 (3) Mohammed gave me some good advice.

القاعدة (5) لا تستخدم أداتي النكرة «a أو an» قبل أسماء الجمع التي تعد. الأمثلة :

 (1) Planes are Faster than trains .

 (2) Teachers like students.

القاعدة (6) : لا تستخدم «a» أو an قبل أسماء الوجبات . الأمثلة :

breakfast, lunch, dinner

استثناءات : إذا سبق اسم الوجبة صفة ، أو إذا كانت وجبة خاصة للاحتفال بمناسبة معينة أو على شرف
شخص ، فتستخدم في هذه الحالة «a» أو «an». الأمثلة :

 : We had a good lunch .

 : Mr Omar invited me to a dinner to welcome the new ambassador.

القاعدة (7) استخدم كلاً من أداتي النكرة a/an قبل الجنسيات والوظائف والمهن . الأمثلة :

a teacher , an ambassador, a Jordanian, an Egyptian .

أداة المعرفة the

القاعدة (8) استخدم أداة المعرفة the للإشارة إلى الأشياء الفريدة في الكون. الأمثلة:

the sun , the moon , the equator , the sky

القاعدة (9) استخدم أداة المعرفة the عند الإشارة إلى شيء محدد مسبقًا أو شيء يعرفه المستمع. الأمثلة :

 : I forgot the contract (a certain contract) on the table (a certain a table)

 : I watched the match (a certain match) yesterday .

القاعدة (10) استخدم أداة المعرفة the قبل أسماء المحيطات والبحار والأنهار والقنوات ومجموعات الجزر وسلاسل الجبال والصحارى والمناطق وأسماء الجمع لبعض الدول . الأمثلة :

The Indies ocean, The Red Sea, The Nile , The Suez Canal, The Bahamas, The Indies , The Sahara, The Middle East, The United States, The Soviet Union.

القاعدة (11) استخدم the قبل أسماء الآلات والأجهزة والآلات الموسيقية. الأمثلة :

the radio , the piano , the photocopier

القاعدة (12) استخدم the قبل الأسماء المفردة للحيوانات والطيور والورود والحشرات والنباتات والأسماك للإشارة إلى الفصيلة بشكل عام . الأمثلة :

: the rose is my favourite flower.

: the whale is the biggest animal.

: the turquoise is my best jewel.

القاعدة (13) استخدم the قبل أسماء الصحف والمجلات . الأمثلة :

The times, The New York Times, The times of India . The gulf Times, The Times (magazine) .

القاعدة (14) استخدم the قبل الصفات التى تشير إلى الطبقة أو المجموعة بشكل عام . الأمثلة :

the poor, (poor people) the rich (rich people)

القاعدة (15) استخدم أداة المعرفة the قبل أسماء الفنادق والمطاعم والحانات والمسارح ودور السينما والمتاحف . الأمثلة :

the Sheraton , the Abu Shaqra (restaurant) , the Royal (cinema), the Egyptian Museum.

القاعدة (16) استخدم أداة المعرفة the قبل الصفات أو قبل الأسماء east , west north, south . الأمثلة :

: The elderly or often lonely.

 The handicapped need access to public building.

 Luxor is in the south .

استثناءات:

South Africa, North America, South America, West Germany,

القاعدة (17) استخدم أداة المعرفة the قبل الصفات التى تشير إلى الجنسية، عند الإشارة إلى شعب إحدى

الدول . الأمثلة :

 : The Sudanese are kind people .

 : The Japanese are active people .

 : The French are famous for their taste.

ملاحظة : مع الجنسيات الأخرى استخدم جمع الاسم الذى يشير للجنسية أى إضافة s إلى الاسم .

القاعدة (18) استخدم the قبل الأماكن والمبانى . الأمثلة :

 : the central bank of Qatar , the great wall of china.

القاعدة (19) استخدم أداة المعرفة the قبل صفات التفضيل . الأمثلة :

 : This is the best cake I have ever eaten.

 china has the largest population of all countries in the world .

 Mr. Everest is the highest mountain in the world.

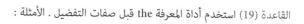 Ahmed Zewail is the first scientist discovered Femtosecond.

ملاحظة : لا تستخدم أداة المعرفة the مع الأعداد الترتيبية عندما تستعمل بمفردها .

الأمثلة :

: She was first in her class.

 : Our team is third in the standing.

القاعدة (20) لا تستخدم أداة المعرفة the قبل كلمة man عندما تشير إلى البشر بوجه عام . الأمثلة :

 : Man can not live without water.

القاعدة : (21) لا تستخدم أداة المعرفة the قبل أسماء الناس . الأمثلة :

 : Nashwa, Talal , Rania, Magda, Yousif

استثناءات : (أ) إذا كان الاسم يشير إلى العائلة فاستخدم أداة المعرفة the. الأمثلة :

 : The Hendersons have moved.

 : The Smiths came this evening.

(ب) تستخدم أداة المعرفة the عند التمييز بين شخص وآخر لهما نفس الاسم . الأمثلة:

 : The George Brown who teaches here is not the George Brown in college.

القاعدة (22) لا تستخدم أداة المعرفة the قبل الأسماء المجردة . الأمثلة :

 : Wisdom is gift of heavens.

 : Honesty is the best policy .

 : Virtue is its own rewards.

استثناءات : تستخدم أداة المعرفة the إذا كان الاسم المجرد يشير إلى شيء أو حالة بعينها . الأمثلة :

 : I can't forget the kindness with which he treated me .

القاعدة (23) لا تستخدم أداة المعرفة the قبل أسماء الألعاب الرياضية. الأمثلة :

 : football, tennis, handball, volleyball.

القاعدة : (24) لا تستخدم أداة المعرفة the قبل أسماء الوجبات . الأمثلة :

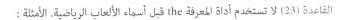

: I had lunch with Mushira.

: I have my breakfast at 7.30 .

القاعدة (25) لا تستخدم أداة المعرفة the قبل أسماء الجمع التى تعد عند استخدامها بشكل عام . الأمثلة :

 : Engineers make good salaries.

 : Children like chocolate .

: Computers are used in every company .

القاعدة (26) لا تستخدم أداة المعرفة the مع أسماء المدن الكبرى والصغرى والقرى .

الأمثلة :

 : Cairo, Doha, Abu Dhabi, Amman , Beirut.

القاعدة (27) لا تستخدم أداة المعرفة the مع أسماء الدول والولايات . الأمثلة :

: Germany , Italy, Jordan, Syria, Egypt, Qatar

استثناءات : (أ) the Yemen , the Sudan

(ب) إذا كان ملحقاً باسم البلد كلمات مثل Republic, Union, Kingdom, states, فاستخدم أداة المعرفة the . الأمثلة :

: The Democratic Republic of China , The Arab Republic of Egypt, The Soviet Union, The United Kingdom, The United States of America.

القاعدة (28) لا تستخدم أداة المعرفة the مع أسماء الجزر التى تتكون من اسم واحد فقط . الأمثلة :

 : Sicily , Bermuda, Japanese, Islands in general.

القاعدة : (29) لا تستخدم أداة المعرفة the قبل أسماء الجبال . الأمثلة :

 Everest, Enta

القاعدة : (30) لا تستخدم أداة المعرفة the قبل أسماء البحيرات . الأمثلة :

Lake Naser , Lake Superior

القاعدة (31) لا تستخدم أداة المعرفة the مع أسماء الشوارع والطرق والميادين .

الأمثلة:

 1000 Fifth Avenue, Murad Street, Tahrir Square.

القاعدة (32) لا تستخدم أداة المعرفة the قبل أى اسم يتكون من كلمتين.

 : Cairo University , Cairo Airport, Ramses Station

استثناءات :

 the Wagba Palace, the Quba palace, the White House.

القاعدة (33) لا تستخدم أداة المعرفة the قبل الألقاب التى يتبعها اسم . الأمثلة :

 : President Mubarak, King Abd Dllah, Princess Diana , Queen Elizabeth .

ملاحظة : تستخدم أداة المعرفة the مع الألقاب التى لا يتبعها اسم . الأمثلة :

 the queen , the president, the prince, the king.

القاعدة (34) لا تستخدم أداة المعرفة the مع الألوان . الأمثلة :

 : I like black.

القاعدة (35) لا تستخدم أداة المعرفة the مع اللغات . الأمثلة :

 : Dalia speaks French.

 : Spanish is my second language.

القاعدة (36) لا تستخدم أداة المعرفة the مع الأديان . الأمثلة :

 : Islam is the right religion.

القاعدة (37) لا تستخدم أداة المعرفة the مع المواد الدراسية . الأمثلة:

 : Mohammed is bad at English.

 : Mahmoud likes mathematics.

القاعدة (38) تستخدم أداة المعرفة the مع أسماء السفن . الأمثلة :

 : The Titanic

القاعدة (39) لا تستخدم أداة المعرفة the مع كلمات المستشفى والجامعة والكلية والمدرسة والسجن والكنيسة عندما تشير هذه الكلمات إلى الغرض الأساسى منها .

الأمثلة:

 : I have to go to hospital because of stomach pain (I'm

sick)

 : I have to go to the hospital to visit Nader.

 : Romel went to church (to pray) .

 : Romel went to the church to repair sound system.

 : Hisham was put in prison (Hisham is criminal)

 : Hisham went to the prison to visit Hani.

القاعدة (40) لا تستخدم أداة المعرفة the مع كلمات مثل home,bed, work. الأمثلة :

 : Sayed went home at 2 a.m yesterday.

 : Shehab is still in bed.

 : Sherif is at work from 9 a.m to 4 p.m.

Possessives
صيغ الملكية

هناك شكلان لتركيب صيغ الملكية ، أحدهما يأتي بعده of وهذا الشكل سهل البنا ، أما التركيب الآخر فهو يأتي بعد 's أو 'و' وهذا الشكل محير في بنائه.

الأسماء Apostrophe + s or apostrophe alone

من الممكن تحويل الأسماء إلى صيغ الملكية من خلال إضافة 's أما إذا كانت الكلمة تنتهي بحرف s فيضاف إلى نهاية الكلمة (') فقط. الأمثلة:

 : The dog's bark. (singular)

 : A day's work. (singular)

 : Curtis' friends (plural)

 : The Johnson' house. (plural)

استخدام of في عبارة بعد أسماء ليست مرتبطة بالناس الأمثلة:

 : The tires of the car.

 : The surface of the road.

التمييز بين صيغ التملك ('s - s')

القاعدة (1) تأخذ الأسماء المتصلة بالناس والنشاط البشري عادة صيغ 's

الأمثلة :

(A) proper name

(أ) للأسماء المعروفة لشخص معين

Amr Moussa's speech.

(B) Personal nouns.

(ب) للإشارة إلى اسم شخص

The girl's dress.

(C) Collective nouns

(ج) للأسماء الجماعية

The teams' success.

(D) Nouns relating to human activity .

(د) للأسماء المتصلة بالنشاط البشرى

The body's ability .

(E) Geographical names

(هـ) للأسماء الجغرافية :

(F) institutioen

(و) للمؤسسات :

The university's budget.

The museum's members.

القاعدة (2) معظم العبارات التى تشير إلى الزمن تأخذ صيغة s'

الأمثلة :

 : a month's pay   two week's vacation

a year's work   season's greetings

القاعدة (3) تأخذ بعض التعبيرات الاصطلاحية صيغة s'

الأمثلة :

 : Our money's worth an arm's length.

القاعدة (4) تأخذ الحيوانات ذات الترتيب الأرقى صيغة s'

: a dog's life   The kitten's cry

The horse's man   The cat's meow

القاعدة (5) قد يحذف الاسم الذى يأتى بعد s' إذا كان هذا السياق يجعل المعنى أكثر وضوحاً .

: (1) Ali's course is harder than Ahmed's (Ahmed's course)

(1) Hassan's dog is well trained, but Fahmi's is not . (Fahmi's dog)

(2) They bought their furniture at El- Iraqi's.

(El-Iraqi's Furniture Store)

القاعدة (6) تستخدم صيغ التملك المضاعفة كلاً من of و s وهى شائعة مع الأسماء المعرفة عندما تكون الإشارة محددة وذات شكل شخصى .

الأمثلة :

 : A novel of Conrad's .

A simphony of Beethoven's .

A friend of my father's .

A painting of Picasso's .

القاعدة (7) نستخدم صيغ الملكية المضاعفة مع الضمائر وهناك صيغتان للإشارة إلى ضمائر الملكية .

(أ) صيغة يقع فيها الضمير قبل الاسم   (ب) صيغة تأتى بعد of

ضمير الملكية الذي يأتي بعد of	صفة الملكية التي يأتي بعدها اسم	ضمائر الفاعل
mine	my	I
his	his	he
hers	her	she
it	it	it
your	your	you
ours	our	we
theirs	their	they

الأمثلة :

 :   My friend   a friend of mine

our friends   Friends of ours

This is my car   This car is mine

القاعدة (8) أضف s إلى الأسماء الشاذة (أى التى لا يضاف s إلى نهايتها).

الأمثلة :

 : Women's hairdresser.

The children's hobbies .

القاعدة (9) إذا كان الاسم المفرد (ليس اسمًا لشخص معروف / معين) ينتهى بـ s فاستخدم s' .

الأمثلة :

 : The witness's testimony.

The duchess's activity .   The empress's love .

The princess's boy friend .

القاعدة (10) إذا كانت صيغة المفرد هى صيغة الجمع بالنسبة لبعض الكلمات ، فاستخدم s' دون النظر

إلى أن هذا الاسم مفرد أو جمع .

الأمثلة :

 : Sheep's wool / glasses's lenses

القاعدة (11) استخدم(s') أو(') فقط فى الجزء الأخير من الكلمات المركبة.

الأمثلة :

 : The baby sitter's money.

Monday, June 15 is Maryan Morgan's birthday.

القاعدة (12) إذا كان هناك شخصان يشتركان فى ملكية شيء ما فاستخدم s' بعد الكلمة الأخيرة .

الأمثلة :

 : Ali and Amira's son. Talal and Rania's father.

القاعدة (13) لا تستخدم apostrophe، عند استخدام العبارة بصيغة وصفية .

الأمثلة :

 : The musicians union.   A technicians committee .

القاعدة (14) استخدم s' مع الأحرف الأولية التى تشير إلى معانى تركيب معين .

الأمثلة :

: GM's decision .

The VIP's reception .

القاعدة (15) استخدم s ' مع ⟵ sake + اسم

الأمثلة :

 : For heaven's sake,   For goodness' sake,

For appearnce's sake, for conscience's sake

القاعدة (16) أحياناً تستخدم s ' مع الناس لتشير إلى منازلهم .

الأمثلة :

 : We will have a party at Ali's (Ali's house)

 : Ahmed's house is older than Mostafa .

القاعدة (17) لا تستخدم apostrophe مع ضمائر الملكية أو الأسماء الموصولة.

الأمثلة :

 : This bicycle is mine .

This is Mr. Ali whose house I live in .

استثناءات : استخدم apostrophe مع الضمائر المبهمة أو غير المحددة .

الأمثلة :

 : One's emotions   Somebody else's idea's

Another's hope.   Everyone's concept.

القاعدة (18) تستخدم كلمة own عادة بعد صفة الملكية ، لتأكيد ملكية المتكلم لشيء ما .

الأمثلة :

 : this is my own car.   This is my own fault.

Nouns
الأسماء

الأسماء هى كلمات تشير إلى الأشياء مثل الإنسان والحيوان والأماكن والأفكار والمؤسسات ، وقد يكون الاسم فاعلاً لجملة وتسمى الأسماء أحياناً بأسماء الذات substantives وهو مصطلح يشير إلى أى كلمة أو مجموعة من الكلمات ، والتى تستخدم كفاعل لجملة أى : اسم أو ضمير ، عبارة اسمية، اسم فاعل (+ v ing) أو عبارة تبدأ بالمصدر .

أنواع الأسماء Kinds of nouns

(1) أسماء تعد وأخرى لا تعد :

(أ) الأسماء التى تعد :

(1) أسماء الأشخاص والحيوانات والنباتات والحشرات وأجزاء تلك الأشياء

Persons	Animals	Plants	Insects	Parts
a boy	a cat	a cactus	an ant	an ankle كاحل
a girl	a dog	a bush	a butterfly	a bone عظمة
a man	a hourse	a flower	a caterpillar	a face وجه

(2) الأشياء التى لها شكل معين

a ball	a car	a house	a street	a typewriter طبّاع
a fluid	a door	a mountain	a tent	an umbrella مظلة

(3) وحدات القياس بأنواعها المختلفة :

a gram	a foot قدم	a square foot قدم مربع	a centimeter	a degree درجة
an inch بوصة	a meter	a cubic inch بوصة مكعبة	a drop	a kind نوع
a type	a piece	a bit	an item	a part جزء

(4) تصنيفات المجتمع :

a family أسرة	a country دولة	a language
a clan عشيرة	a state دولة	a word
a tribe قبيلة	a city	a phrase

(5) بعض الأسماء المجردة :

a help	an invitation	a rest
a hindrance	a nuisance إزعاج	a word
an idea	a plan	a taboo محظور - محرّم

(ب) الأسماء التي لا تعد :

(1) أسماء المواد

Natural Qualities	Material and Metals	food
lightness إضاءة	copper نحاس	bread خبز
darkness ظلام	cotton قطن	cake كعكة
heaviness ثقل	dacron داكرون	chocolate شيكولاته
dullness بلاهم	grass عشب	meat لحم
adolescence سن المراهقة	iron حديد	spaghetti سباجيتي
	wood خشب	spinach سبانخ

(2) أسماء السوائل والغازات والخلاصات التى تتكون من أشياء صغيرة .

Natural Qualities	Material and Metals	food
coffee	air	barley
milk	oxygen	rice

(3) الأسماء المتعلقة باللغات :

: Arabic, English , Chinese, Japanese, French... etc

(4) معظم الكلمات التى تنتهى بـ ing :

تخييم camping	مشى لمسافة طويلةhiking	موقف سيارات parking
كسوة clothing	learning التعلم	تسوق shopping
دانسينج dancing رقص	lightning برق	smoking تدخين

استثناءات : نستثنى من هذه القاعدة الكلمات الآتية :

building, feeling, dealing , wedding

* كلمة helping عندما نعنى حصة من الطعام .

* كلمة saving فهى تعنى الادخار أما كلمة savings فتعنى المدخرات.

* كلمة furnishings (تجهيزات أو أثاث) دائماً جمع .

(5) العديد من الأسماء المجردة والتى تلحق بها النهايات الآتية

ness, ance , ence , ity

الأمثلة :

beauty جمال	ignorance جهل	serenity صفاء
equality مساواة	selfishness أنانية	happiness سعادة

(6) العديد من الكلمات التى تجمع فى اللغات الأخرى لا تجمع فى اللغة الإنجليزية .

الأمثلة :

advice نصيحة	leisure فراغ	damage	rubbish نفاية
behavior سلوك	luck حظ	conduct	violence عنف
money مال	courage شجاعة	poetry	weather طقس
news أخبار	luggage أمتعة	progress	photography تصوير

(7) عند تصنيف الكلمات التى لا تعد تأتى بعد of .

الأمثلة:

:   a piece of cake   an amount of leisure

a slice of bread   five pound of sugar

a bottle of milk   a yard of cloth

ملحوظة :

كلمات مثل piece و bit يمكن استخدامها مع العديد من الكلمات ، ولكن الكلمات المشابهة الأخرى

تستخدم فقط مع عدد قليل من الأسماء التى لا تعد.

الأمثلة :

a slice of bread / cake / meat .

a blade of grass / wheat .

a bar of chocolate / copper / candy .

a grain of rice / barley / wheat .

a sheet of paper / ice .

a lump of coal / sugar.

(8) العديد من الكلمات التى قد تعد أو لا تعد ، فالمواد والأنشطة والأفكار المجردة قد تعد حينما نشير إلى

بند أو مثال بعينه .

الأمثلة :

Countable	Uncountable
an activity , activities	activity
an agreement , agreements	agreement
an art, arts	art
a beauty , beauties	beauty
a brick, bricks	brick (substance)

a brick, bricks	bone (substance)
a business, buisnesses	business (activity)
a cake , cakes	cake (substance)
a chocolate, chocolates	chocolate (substance

** أسماء الجنس / شبيهة الجمع Collective Nouns

تشير أسماء الجنس إلى نوع خاص من الأسماء التى قد تتصف به مجموعة من الناس أو الحيوانات أو الطيور أو الحشرات، وقد يتبع تلك الأسماء فعل فى المفرد أو الجمع وهذا يعتمد على صيغة الاسم ذاته ، فإذا كان يشير كوحدة واحدة لمعناه ففى هذه الحالة يكون الفعل فى صيغة المفرد ، أما إذا كان يشير إلى أفراد وحدة الاسم ، ففى هذه الحالة يكون الفعل فى الجمع .
الأمثلة :

* بعض أسماء الجنس التى تشير للناس هى:

army جيش	choir جوقة	congregation مجمع	police شرطة
audience جمهور	chorus كوراس	group مجموعة	team فريق
band فرقة	clan عشيرة	orchestra فرقة موسيقية	troop قوة
brigade لواء	class فصل	patrol دورية	youth شباب

* بعض أسماء الجنس التى تشير للحيوانات والطيور والحشرات هى :

A herd of cattle / sheep / goats   A hive of bees

A flock of birds / chikens   A swarm of ants / bees flies

كيفية تحويل الاسم المفرد إلى جمع

القاعدة (1) تجمع معظم الأسماء فى الإنجليزية بإضافة s - إلى نهاية الاسم المفرد:

الأمثلة :

 :

| car | cars | finger | fingers |
| boy | boys | book | books |

القاعدة (2) أضف es إلى الأسماء المفردة التى تنتهى بالنهايات التالية :

sh, ch , ss, s, o , x

(2) أسماء الأعلام وهى تشير إلى أشخاص بعينهم أو أماكن بعينها وتكتب بحروف كبيرة، وفيما عدا ذلك هى أسماء عامة أو نكرة.

Examples:

Monday, June 15, is Rania Mahmoud's birthday

Farouk al Baz studied at George Washington University Osama Al - Baz studied at Cairo University .

ملحوظة : يسبق أسماء الأعلام أدوات إذا اتفق اسم الشخص مع اسم المكان أو الشيء.

 : My brother is named Saad El-Wialy and my cousin also named Saad el Wialy .

The Saad El - Wialy who lives acorss the street from is my brother .

القاعدة (2)

* يمكن تصنيف الأسماء النكرة أو العامة إلى:

(ب) أسماء مادية أو ذاتية   (أ) أسماء مجردة

الأسماء المجردة :

(A) Abstract nouns :

وهى التى تشير إلى الأفكار والعواطف والصفات المميزة أو الحالات .

: justice عدل, beauty جمال , happiness سعادة, length طول, classification تصنيف.

(ب) الأسماء المادية أو الذاتية : Concrete Nouns

 : boy , bread , chair , noise , fire , smoke , water , etc .

A war , wars (a particular War (activity examples)

A wine, wines (a kind of) Wine substance

A work , works (of art , of an Work (effort) author

A worry , worries (one or more worry (activity)

examples)

(9) بعض الكلمات التى لها صيغ متشابهة ، إحداهما تعد والأخرى لا تعد.

Countable	Uncountable
clothes ثياب- جمع فقط	clothing
dance رقص	dancing
furnishings جمع فقط- تأثيث	furniture
laugh (s) ضحك	laughter , laughing
machine (s) آلة	machinary
moonbeam (s) شعاع القمر	moonlight
payment (s) سداد	pay
permit (s) رخصة	permission
sunbeam (s) شعاع الشمس	sunlight
use (s) استخدام	usefulness

(10) تتحول بعض الكلمات من أسماء لا تعد إلى أسماء تعد أو العكس عند إضافة بادئة ببداية الكلمة .

Countabe	Uncountable
indecision	decision (abstraction)
inequality, inequalities	equality (abstraction)
justice (s) person only)	justice (abstraction)
	injustice (abstraction)
an injustice , injustice	

Countable	Uncountable
xloth, cloths	cloth (substance)
a decision, decisions	decision
a duty , duties	duty
a fire, fires	fire (substance)
a hair, hairs	hair (substance)
a history, histories	history (study in the past)
an honor , honors	honor (absrtact)
a hope, hopes	hope (abstract)
an iron, iron	iron (c)
a kinkdness,	kindness (abstract)
a language, languages	language (activity)
a light, lights	light (substance)
a material , materials	material
a noise, noises	noise
a pain , pains	pain (collective)
paper , papers	paper (substance)
a pity	pity (emotion)
a pleasure, pleasures	pleasure
a silence , silence (a period of periods of time without sounds)	silence (lack of sound)
a space , space (empty place or places.	space
a stone, stones (a piece or pieces)	stone (substance)
a success, success	success (abstraction)
a thought, thoughts	thought (abstraction)
a time, times (an occassion, occasions)	time (collective)

Countabe	Uncountable
a trade, trades (a skill on exchange)	trade (business)
a traffic, traffica (dealing, dealings)	traffic (the number of vehicles)

 : الأمثلة

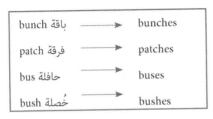

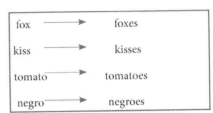

القاعدة (3):

** إذا انتهى الاسم بحرف (y) مسبوقا بحرف متحرك فأضف s ولكن إذا انتهى الاسم بحرف y مسبوقا

بحرف ساكن ، فاحذف y وأضف ies عند التحويل إلى الجمع

Vowel before - y		Consonant before - y	
pay	pays	berry	berries التوت
buy	buys	bury	buries قبر
day	days	try	tries
guy	guys	satisfy	satisfies

القاعدة (4):

** إذا انتهى الاسم المفرد بـ (f) أو (fe) عند التحويل إلى الجمع نحول (f) أو (fe) إلى ves- .

Noun in f , fe	Consonant before-f
calf عجل	calves
belief إيمان	beliefs استثناء
elf قزم	elves
half نصف	halves

life حياة	lives
wife زوجة	wives
knife	knives
proof	proofs استثناء
cliff	cliffs استثناء

** صيغ جمع تختلف عن القواعد السابقة (جمع شاذ):

Examples :

man رجل ⟶ men رجال   child طفل ⟶ children

أطفال

woman امرأة ⟶ women   ox ثور ⟶ oxen ثيران

نسوة

fireman ⟶ firemen   brother أخ ⟶ brethren

رجل مطافي   رجال إطفاء   إخوة

workman ⟶ workmen   foot قدم ⟶ feet أقدام

عامل   عمال

louse   lice قمل   tooth سنة ⟶ teeth أسنان

قـــمـــلـــة

goose وزة ⟶ geese أوز

** القاعدة (6): هناك بعض الأسماء تنتهى بحرف s وهى لا تحمل صيغة الجمع .

Examples : physics, economics , news , ethics .

** القاعدة (7): عند تحويل الأسماء المركبة إلى صيغة الجمع نضيف حرف -s إلى الكلمة الأخيرة.

Examples :

girl - friend رفيقة   girl - friends

grown - up ناضج   grown ups

travel - agents   وكيل سفر   travel - agent

استثناءات : إذا كان الاسم المركب يتكون من الشق الأول رجل أو امرأة، ففهى هذه الحالة نجمع كلاً من الاسمين.

Examples :

man driver   men drivers

woman driver   women drivers

نضيف s إلى الشق الأول للاسم المركب ، إذا كانت الصيغة تتكون من (فعل + er + ظرف)

 الأمثلة :

runners - up   fillers - in

passers - by

(جـ) إضافة s إلى الشق المركب من الاسم المركب والذى يتكون من

noun + preposition + noun

: works of art   sisters - in - law

القاعدة (8):

* تستخدم صيغة الفعل فى المفرد مع بعض أسماء الجمع التى تشير للمال ومدة من الوقت والمسافة .. إلخ .

: Eighty pounds is not enough to buy a good watch .

Ten days is not enough to see Japan .

القاعدة (9):

** تستخدم بعض الأسماء التى تشير إلى أجزاء من الملبس أو بعض الأدوات فى صيغة الجمع .

: glasses, shorts, sciessors, trousers, shoes

ملحوظة : يمكن استخدام a pair of مع هذه الكلمات

A pair of glasses   A pair of shoes.

القاعدة (10):

** القاعدة نستخدم أداة المعرفة the مع بعض الصفات لإضفاء صيغة الجمع عليها.

Ex: The strong (strong people) find (discover) their way in life .

القاعدة (11):

** القاعدة هناك تصنيف خاص بالكلمات ذات الأصل اليوناني أو اللاتيني حسب القواعد اليونانية أو
اللاتينية عند التحويل من المفرد إلى الجمع .

Examples :

ae تتحول a	amoeba	amoebae الأميبا	
	antenna	antennae هوائي	
a تتحول on	phenomenon	phenomena ظاهرة	
es تتحول إلى is	oasis	oases واحة	
	thesis	theses أطروحة	
a تتحول إلى um	bacterium	bacteria جرثوم	
	curriculum	curricula منهج	
i تتحول إلى us	cactus	cacti صبار	
	stimulus	stimuli حافز	

القاعدة (12):

** بعض الأسماء دائماً في صيغة الجمع ولا يسبقها أي رقم .

Exmples :

credentials أوراق اعتماد , auspices رعاية, grounds أراض , stairs

congratulations, ملابس clothes, متاع belongings, سجلات archives سجلات الأحداث, annals سلام
odds حبوبة, misgivings أخلاق manners (appearance) مظاهر looks , أرباح earnings , تهاني
خلافات particular, (details) تفاصيل خاصة premises , عائدات proceeds , أرباع quarters , (place
to live), regards تحيات , remains بقايا, resources موارد, riches أغنياء shortcomings أوجه قصور,
suds رغاوي الصابون, surroundings تخوم, thanks تشكرات, valuables أشياء ثمينة, whereabouts
أماكن الحدوث .

القاعدة (13):

** بعض الأسماء لها صيغة جمع ولكنها تحمل معنى الاسم المفرد، ويأتي بعدها الفعل في المفرد .

checkers (draught) لعبة الداما	series سلسلة
Chess الشطرنج	molasses دبس السكر
econimics علم الاقتصاد	mumps التهاب الغدة النكفية
mathematics رياضيات	news أخبار
means وسائل	physics فيزياء
measles الحصبة	statistics إحصائات
metropolis مدينة/عاصمة	tennis التنس

القاعدة (14):

** القاعدة معظم الأسماء التي تنتهي بـ th يتم جمعها حسب المعتاد أي بإضافة s إلى نهاية الكلمة .

Nouns in th	Plural
breath تنفس	breaths
cloth قماش	cloths
wreath إكليل	wreaths

(1) Alice Maclin Reference Guide to English   A Hand Book of English as a second language , United States. Information Agency , Washington, D.C 20547, the Materials Branch , English Language Division. Mc Arthur and Berly Atkins .

(2) Tom York Dictionary of phrasal Verbs and Their Idioms, Egyptian International Publishing Company, Longman.

(3) Michael Braganza, Common Errors In English , New Delhi, 1998 Goodwill Publishing House.

(4) إيهاب صبيح محمد زريق، القاموس الشامل فى الأفعال المركبة - القاهرة - دار الكتب العلمية للنشر والتوزيع .

(5) حسن سعيد الكرمى، المغنى الأكبر (إنجليزى - عربى)، بيروت، مكتبة لبنان .

INDEX

ENGLISH
WITHOUT
MISTAKES

Printed in the United States
By Bookmasters